Unexpected Bravery
Women and Children of the Civil War

A. J. Schenkman

Globe
Pequot

Guilford, Connecticut

Globe Pequot

An imprint of Globe Pequot, the trade division of
The Rowman & Littlefield Publishing Group, Inc.
4501 Forbes Blvd., Ste. 200
Lanham, MD 20706
www.rowman.com

Distributed by NATIONAL BOOK NETWORK

British Library Cataloguing in Publication Information available

Library of Congress Cataloging-in-Publication Data

Names: Schenkman, A. J., author.
Title: Unexpected bravery : women and children of the Civil War / A.J.
  Schenkman.
Description: Guilford, Connecticut : Globe Pequot, [2021] | Includes
  bibliographical references. | Summary: "What is little known about the
  American Civil War is that both women and children enlisted in an
  attempt to make a difference in the struggle to determine the future of
  the United States of America"— Provided by publisher.
Identifiers: LCCN 2021026126 (print) | LCCN 2021026127 (ebook) | ISBN
  9781493055265 (trade paperback) | ISBN 9781493055272 (epub)
Subjects: LCSH: Women and war—United States—History—19th century. |
  Children and war—United States—History—19th century. | United
  States—History—Civil War, 1861-1865—Participation, Female. | United
  States—History—Civil War, 1861-1865—Women—Biography. | United
  States—History—Civil War, 1861-1865—Participation, Juvenile. | United
  States—History—Civil War, 1861-1865—Children—Biography.
Classification: LCC E628 .S45 2021 (print) | LCC E628 (ebook) | DDC
  973.7082—dc23
LC record available at https://lccn.loc.gov/2021026126
LC ebook record available at https://lccn.loc.gov/2021026127

Dedicated to
Jonah G. Schenkman

The horrors of the battlefield were brought vividly before me. I joined a detachment which was collecting the dead for burial. Sickening at the sights, I made my way with another detachment, which was gathering the wounded, to a log house which had been appropriated for a hospital. Here the scenes were so terrible that I became faint, and making my way to a tree, sat down, the most woebegone twelve year old in America.

—FRED GRANT, THEN TWELVE YEARS OLD
AND SON OF THEN LT. GEN. ULYSSES S. GRANT,
DESCRIBING THE SCENE AT VICKSBURG, MISSISSIPPI.
QUOTED FROM "A BOY'S EXPERIENCE AT VICKSBURG."

Grant family with Fred Grant on horseback
LIBRARY OF CONGRESS

CONTENTS

Acknowledgments vii
Introduction: Children and Women During Wartime. 1

PART I: CHILDREN SOLDIERS OF THE CIVIL WAR
CHAPTER 1: Johnny Clem (The Drummer Boy
of Chickamauga) 7
CHAPTER 2: Susie King Taylor (Nurse and Teacher) 20
CHAPTER 3: Charles Whipple Hadley (Bravery at Shiloh) 33
CHAPTER 4: The Howe Brothers (Orion and Lyston) 45
CHAPTER 5: William H. Horsfall (Medal of Honor) 60
CHAPTER 6: Alexander H. Johnson (Drummer for
the 54th) 65
CHAPTER 7: Lola Sanchez (Confederate Spy) 71
CHAPTER 8: Unfinished Lives, Part I 74

PART II: WOMEN SOLDIERS OF THE CIVIL WAR
CHAPTER 9: Albert D. J. Cashier (Jennie Hodgers) 89
CHAPTER 10: Mary Galloway (Wounded at Antietam) 107
CHAPTER 11: Florena Budwin (Woman Prisoner at
Andersonville). 111
CHAPTER 12: Cathay Williams (William Cathay) 115
CHAPTER 13: Mary Owens Jenkins (John Evans) 121
CHAPTER 14: Elizabeth "Lizzie" Compton
(Johnny "Jack" Compton). 126
CHAPTER 15: Sarah Malinda Pritchard Blalock (Sam Blalock) . . . 131
CHAPTER 16: Sarah Emma Edmonds (Franklin Thompson) 142

Contents

Chapter 17: Loreta Janeta Velazquez (Harry T. Buford) 153
Chapter 18: Unfinished Lives, Part II 163

Bibliography 175
About the Author 191

ACKNOWLEDGMENTS

I WOULD LIKE TO THANK Dave Joens, Illinois State Archives; the Worcester Public Library; the Worcester Historical Museum; Annakathryn Welch, archivist, Archives of Michigan, Michigan History Center; Megan Klintworth, iconographer, Abraham Lincoln Presidential Library and Museum; Ross Cooper, public services specialist, Special Collections Research Center, Belk Library and Information Commons, Appalachian State University; Amy Lyons, editor, Globe Pequot/ Rowman and Littlefield; Alyssa Messenger; Mary Mannix; Tracey McIntire; Dr. Audry Scanlan-Teller; Russell Horton, reference outreach archivist, Wisconsin Veterans Museum; Terry Reimer, National Museum of Civil War Medicine; Mallory Herberger, Special Collections archivist, Maryland Historical Society; Anita Hoffman, archivist, Heritage Frederick, Maryland; Michelle Greco; Jonah Schenkman; Amy Vedra, director of reference services, Indiana Historical Society; Michael Vetman, archivist, Indiana Archives and Records Administration; Gail Lelyveld; Kerry George, Wayne County Historical Museum; Steve Barrett, Marion County historian; L. Tom Perry, Special Collections, Brigham Young University; Allison Johnson, Becki Plunkett, Special Collections archivist/ coordinator, and Hang Nguyen, PhD, musicologist and reference librarian, all at the State Historical Society of Iowa; National Archives and Records Administration, Washington, DC; Library of Congress, Washington, DC; SUNY New Paltz; Anna Pivora, executive director, and Chris Gardner, curator of collections, Crawford Collection, Boone County Museum of History; National Park Service; Vicksburg National Military Park and Antietam Battlefield; Gretchen Weerheim, J. J. Blickstein; Joakim Lartey; Keicha Kempsey; Melissa Kimler-Alm; Stephanie Phillips, North Carolina State Archives; Teddy Yoder, Esq., Campbell County Historical & Genealogical Society, and Ellen Urban.

INTRODUCTION:
CHILDREN AND WOMEN DURING WARTIME

WHEN I WAS A LITTLE BOY, MY MOTHER AND FATHER PUT MY BROTHER and the family dog into the Jeep Cherokee Chief. We stopped for breakfast at a local diner on Main Street in Kew Gardens Hills in Queens County, New York, where I grew up. We were embarking on a two-week adventure with the aim of viewing as many of the major Civil War battlefields as we could in that period of time. Some four decades later, I still remember Gettysburg. The open fields of Gettysburg, the turning point in the Civil War, became indelibly etched in my psyche. A park ranger explained to my family the number of soldiers involved and the carnage of the battlefield.

A fourteen-year-old Confederate killed by a bayonet at Fort Mahone
"PORTRAIT OF BOY SOLDIER"/LIBRARY OF CONGRESS

I

Today you can still feel the energy of the souls who fought and perished on that great field of battle from July 1 to July 3, 1863. Nowhere else have I felt that energy, possibly with the exception of Pearl Harbor, standing above the sunken remains of the USS *Arizona*. I still remember the "tears" of the soldier who perished on December 7, 1941, manifesting as oil slowly making its way to the top of Pearl Harbor one drop at a time.

These battles in the Civil War were led by great men like Generals Robert E. Lee and George G. Meade. The battles were fought by average or less than average individuals who struggled and, in some cases, died or lived the rest of their lives in relative anonymity. It is these ordinary soldiers about whom I strive to know more so, as President Abraham Lincoln stated in his Gettysburg Address, "that these dead shall not have died in vain. . . ."

Unexpected Bravery examines the lives of women and children soldiers of the Civil War. Historians know that roughly six hundred thousand soldiers perished during the Civil War, which lasted from 1861 to 1865—this out of a US population of thirty-two million. Of this thirty-two million, roughly four million were human beings owned as property. Researchers believe that close to three million individuals served in the Civil War. Historians maintain that about four hundred women disguised themselves as men to serve in the Civil War. They joined for many reasons, including being with husbands, brothers, or lovers; adventure; patriotism; to end slavery; and money. These reasons were not always mutually exclusive.

Even though it was illegal for women to serve in the armed forces, let alone dress like men, they could still escape detection. Most of the time, when they were discovered, it was because of a wound or in death. Some were never discovered and simply left the army before or after the war. Some women wrote about their experiences, while others just resumed their lives in society as women. In the case of Albert D. J. Cashier, he continued to live and identify as a man.

The legal age to join the army during the Civil War was age eighteen. This did not deter some two hundred thousand underage boys and girls from entering both the Union and the Confederate armies. Many joined as drummer boys, alongside their fathers or older brothers. Still others joined by just tagging along with troops on the move. Susie Baker Taylor King joined as a nurse and laundress for the army. Women disguised as men joined the army for a sense of adventure, because of a bad home life, to help end slavery, for the money, or to be close to loved ones. Some simply ran away when their guardians refused to give consent.

While researching this book, I learned that almost all of these individuals were significantly affected by the Civil War, most likely suffering from what we might label today as post-traumatic stress disorder or PTSD. In many ways, this war forever changed their lives, as is articulated by Fred Grant in this book's epigraph. Some succumbed to the injuries and trauma that followed them after the war.

This book is quite possibly the most difficult I have ever written. The Civil War was a literate war, meaning that there are many letters, diaries, and memoirs available to the researcher that provide a real feel for the people and the war itself. The war was also covered in the newspapers and by photographers. Detailed military pensions or medical discharges also paint a portrait, again in some instances, of lifelong disabilities both mental and physical from the effects of war.

Finally, this book was written and researched during the COVID-19 pandemic. I could not have completed this book without those institutions and individuals who still did their best to accommodate me even though they were closed. I wrote while remote teaching, remote learning with my son, and being a husband, father, and first responder. I wrote at odd times, most of the time very late at night with a pot of coffee.

Enjoy!

Part I

Children Soldiers of the Civil War

Chapter One

Johnny Clem
(The Drummer Boy of Chickamauga)

Johnny Clem must have wished he never left home and that his father, Roman Klem, would walk through the prison door to take him back home to Newark, Ohio. What enabled Clem to keep going was his hatred for the Rebels who imprisoned him. He could forgive them for confiscating his purse and robbing him of the twenty-five cents it contained. He could not find it in his heart to forgive them for taking his beloved forager cap with three bullet holes from the Battle of Chickamauga. His sheer determination to live allowed him to survive while fellow soldiers sick and starving perished around him. Eventually, the Confederate military authorities paroled the boy Union soldier who, for many, was believed to be the youngest soldier in the war.

John Joseph Klem was born on August 13, 1851, to Roman and Magdalene Klem. He was their first child, and Herman E. Mattingly in *The Family of Johnny Clem* writes that the couple had him "baptized in St. Francis De Sales Church, Newark, Ohio." The year before Johnny was born, Roman was listed in the 1850 US Federal Census as a laborer. Johnny was followed by a sister named Mary Elizabeth (Lizzie) in 1853, and in 1855, his brother Louis was born. Roman, by 1860, was recorded in the census as a gardener. In other words, the family grew vegetables and went around the community selling them. The same year a horrific tragedy affected the family.

Sgt. John Lincoln Clem
"JOHN L. CLEM"/LIBRARY OF CONGRESS

On August 2, 1860, young Clem's mother was killed instantly when she, Mattingly writes, "was hit by a train while she was crossing the railroad in Newark," while trying to avoid another train that was coming straight toward her. Johnny's mother was buried shortly after in Mount Calvary Cemetery in Newark, Licking County, Ohio. With three young children, Roman married soon after his wife's death. His new wife's name was Elizabeth Eckelmier. They married in January 1862. There is no real indication of how Johnny felt toward his new mother. According to Doug Stout of the Veterans Project for the Licking County Library, the family lived at the southeast corner of 11th Street and Granville Street. There are indications that he did not want to remain in the home. The Civil War afforded him that way out.

According to one story, Johnny Clem attempted to become a drummer in Capt. Leonidas McDougal's 3rd Ohio Volunteer Infantry. McDougal refused to enlist him because he was just ten years old. He dismissed Johnny telling him that "he was not enlisting infants." Other stories relate that before Johnny could enlist with the 3rd Ohio, his father located his son and hauled him back home. Many years later, Johnny Clem remembered that his father was dead set against him running off to join the army. It is safe to say his father thought ten years old was too young to join the military in any capacity. Johnny Clem did not allow himself to be deterred. He explained that "the spirit of adventure had gripped me." The youngster was not interested in school and became determined to do everything he could to join the army to save the Union. He tried to enlist again when the 22nd Michigan Volunteer Infantry came through Newark, although Clem remembered that he hopped a train with the 3rd Ohio. When he arrived at Cincinnati, he offered his services as a drummer to the 22nd Michigan Regiment, this time successfully.

The 22nd Michigan Regiment was organized in Pontiac, Michigan. It was mustered into the Union army on August 29, 1862. Moses Wisner, a former governor of the state, became the colonel. The 22nd was created out of General Order No. 154 by Governor Austin Blair, which directed the raising of six regiments of infantry through the Militia Act of 1862. When Clem finally "enlisted," he would be attached to Company C. His immediate officers for Company C were Capt. John Atkinson,

1st Lt. Jefferson J. Wilder, and 2nd Lt. John Sackett. The regiment was camping on the fairgrounds in Pontiac when it received orders to leave for Kentucky on September 4, 1862. They marched to the railroad depot and took the train to Detroit, Michigan. After arriving, later that evening, Clem's future comrades boarded a boat for Cleveland, arriving on September 6, 1862, in Cincinnati, Ohio. Eventually, the 22nd crossed the Ohio River into Covington, Kentucky. It is here that John Clem "joined" the 22nd. He is not recorded in the muster rolls for the 22nd Michigan because the *Denton Record* stated, "He stowed away in a barrage car bound for the Covington, Ky mobilization camp where he attached himself to the 22nd Michigan Infantry." When he was discovered, the soldiers decided to let the boy remain because of his determination.

Clem wrote later in life that "the Civil War was largely a boys' war, one might say. Three out of every ten soldiers on the Union side were under twenty-one years of age." Although the law prevented those under eighteen from joining the army, he maintained that many individuals under eighteen could join, like himself.

His sister remembered another part of the story about her brother absconding and joining the 22nd Michigan. She recounted many years later, when her brother was already a celebrity, that "Johnny had gone to church with his younger sister and brother, probably to evening devotions." Johnny left his siblings there with some excuse for not entering the church with them. She remembered that he told his brother and sister he wanted to go for a swim. The next time she claimed she saw him was two years later.

When the younger children returned home without Johnny, his father searched for him. He was as determined to find his oldest son as his oldest son was not to be found. Johnny managed to avoid Roman and finally became a drummer for the 22nd Michigan. Johnny remembered that even though he was not formally enlisted on the muster rolls, he still earned $13 a month. His fellow soldiers in Company C every pay period took up a collection to pay their beloved drummer boy. It is believed that during this period, Johnny changed his middle name from Joseph to Lincoln in admiration of President Abraham Lincoln. Also, he changed his last name to a more anglicized Clem from Klem. He became known to everyone as John Lincoln Clem.

In an article written by John L. Clem many years after the war, he remembered that he donned a "soldier's uniform, cut down by the regimental tailor from a man's size." His writings, it is essential to point out, are in some respects, suspect. One cannot be sure if he remembered correctly or wanted to make his role in the war more sensational. One such example that has come under scrutiny involves the Battle of Shiloh. The 22nd was mustered into service in August 1862; this would be after the Battle of Shiloh, which was fought April 6-7, 1862. Greg Povelka expands on this "padding of his service record" *in Civil War Times Illustrated*. Povelka believes that Clem's claim that a fragment of a shell smashed his little drum at Shiloh is simply not accurate. "If John beat the drum at Shiloh, it was not with the 22nd Michigan." Povelka maintains that the 3rd Ohio was not at Shiloh either. Some believe that Clem might have remembered his company wrong and that he was briefly with the 3rd Ohio.

It did not stop Clem from perpetuating the Shiloh myth. The *New York Times* reported that "at Shiloh, where Albert Sidney Johnston was killed and where Grant's fame as a soldier began, Clem received his baptism of fire." The story continues that Clem was in the heart of the battle when a Confederate shell exploded close to him. A fragment of the exploding shell destroyed his drum, and the ten-year-old was knocked unconscious. Clem claims that a fellow soldier referred to him as Johnny Shiloh.

"From the fall of 1862 to the spring of 1862, the 22d Michigan was stationed in Kentucky. It divided its time between garrison duty in various Kentucky towns and pursuing cavalry raiders." They also guarded trains and their valuable supplies. They finally left the area by April 1, 1863, when the 22nd was sent to Nashville, Tennessee. The 22nd was mainly on garrison duty. According to Johnny Clem's service records housed in the National Archives, he officially mustered into the 22nd in Nashville, Tennessee, on May 1, 1863. It was easier to track Clem after this official enlistment. He signed on for three years with J. Atkinson, who wrote he was "4 feet tall, with a light complexion blue eyes and light hair." His rank was private. He was twelve years old. During this time, the

22nd continued as part of its duties to protect Union trains and supplies. They also pursued Confederates ending in the occasional skirmish. The 22nd's first significant engagement would be in the Battle of Chickamauga in Georgia. It would be one of the bloodiest single days of fighting in the Western Theater of operations during the Civil War. Chickamauga would make Pvt. John Clem a celebrity after the engagement, earning him the name the Drummer Boy of Chickamauga.

During the middle of September 1863, Maj. Gen. William Rosecrans marched from the middle of Tennessee to capture Chattanooga, Tennessee, which was considered the Confederacy's gateway. Major General Rosecrans wanted to drive Confederate general Braxton Bragg from Chattanooga. The Confederate army withdrew toward Georgia, with both armies skirmishing much of the time. The battle began on September 18, 1863, when General Bragg's Army of the Tennessee attempted to cross Chickamauga Creek and was prevented from doing so by Major General Rosecrans's Army of the Cumberland.

On September 19, 1863, skirmishing developed into a full-scale battle. The next morning on September 20, 1863, John Cohasey, in his book on the 22nd Michigan Infantry, writes that "Bragg reorganized the Army of Tennessee, placing General Longstreet, arriving with the Army of Northern Virginia, and took command of the left wing of the army, and Lt. General Leonidas Polk took command of the right wing." The opening salvos of the battle commenced by 9:30 a.m. Chickamauga changed from a Union advantage, when General Longstreet, with fresh troops, realized there was an opening in the Federal line. It is believed that Major General Rosecrans gave conflicting orders to Maj. Gen. Thomas J. Wood. In response Wood created an opening in the Federal line by moving his troops north. Longstreet took full advantage of the hole created in the Union line of defense. The center collapsed.

Maj. Gen. George Thomas, later given the moniker "the Rock of Chickamauga," was able to rally his troops, holding off the Confederates and preventing the annihilation of the Union troops in retreat. According to John Cohassey, in his book *The 22nd Michigan and the Road to Chickamauga*, Brig. Gen. Gordon Granger, "without direct orders, joined the troops of Major-General Thomas to save the Union left flank." The

John L. Clem and his brother

22nd Michigan, the 21st and the 89th Ohio stood their ground on what became known as the 3rd Hill on Horseshoe Ridge. This allowed the majority of the Union army to withdraw to the safety of Chattanooga. Eventually, the defenders of Horseshoe Ridge were surrounded by the Confederates. Most of the 22nd were captured.

Private Clem, years later, in an autobiographical article written in 1914 entitled *From Nursery to Battlefield* stated, "I went into the battle seated on a caisson alongside of an artilleryman." Sometimes drummer boys were needed to carry weapons. Clem remembered having a musket during the battle and not a drum. His reasoning for shedding his drum was summed up, "I did not like to stand and be shot at without shooting back." Johnny Clem was not a tall child, so carrying a regular musket would be too large for him. "I carried a musket, the barrel of which had been sawed off to a length suitable to my size." When the majority of the 22nd Michigan was captured, Clem was not with his company. In a *New York Times* article from 1915, Clem described that "he came out of the woods like a scared rabbit and ran full tilt into a Confederate Colonel." Laughing at the apparent age of the private, the colonel mockingly ordered Clem to surrender. Private Clem refused, and, in an instant, he leveled his musket on the colonel astride his horse. Clem's rifle exploded, and the unnamed colonel toppled off his horse. While soldiers were falling back, he saw his chances of escape were low. When the Confederates were advancing, he believed his best option for evading capture was to "lay dead until after dark" when Clem thought it was safe enough to continue his retreat back to Union lines. But apparently he did not return immediately to his regiment.

In his service record, it lists Clem as missing. During this time, 1st Lt. Louis Brown of Company C wrote a letter inquiring about Clem's whereabouts. He noted that Clem had been missing since September 20 and was considered by the regiment to be absent without leave (AWOL). It was believed that Private Clem was in Cincinnati, Ohio. Perhaps traumatized by the battle, he went home to recuperate. His sister remembered her brother telling her that he had been wounded during the Battle of Chickamauga. She believed he still had a shell fragment lodged in his hip from that battle.

Johnny Clem does not shed any real light on the issue of why he "disappeared." However, when he did return, because of his bravery during the battle, Private Clem was commissioned a sergeant. This new rank made him the youngest noncommissioned officer in the Union army at the age of twelve. Proud of his new status, Clem not only told his story but showed off his unique souvenir: his forager cap with three musket ball holes in it. He intended on keeping that cap for the rest of his life. Sgt. John Lincoln Clem still had more adventures the next month in October 1863.

Sergeant Clem became a Confederate prisoner of war when, according to the *Newark Advocate*, he was "captured in a raid on a baggage train on October 6, 1863, between Chattanooga and Bridgeport, Ala." Company C's military return listed him as missing in action (MIA) or a prisoner of war (POW). When apprehended, "my captors had no sympathetic interest in Yankee babies in uniform. They stole my jacket; they stole my shoes; they even stole my cap, which I was most anxious to reserve, on account of the bullet holes." If this were not enough of a humiliation, Clem's captors tormented him because of his age. In an autobiographical article, he remembered that one of his tormentors was General "Joe" Wheeler. Much to his anger, Clem became a source of propaganda for the Confederacy. Newspapers reported the Union's apparent desperation to press such young boys into the war. He found the experience insulting and it only increased his hatred for the Rebels.

Clem recollected that he was a prisoner of war for two months, but some historians maintain that it was much less than that. His sister believed that her brother was taken prisoner in Georgia. After he was exchanged, he came home for a week. While he was recuperating from his ordeal, the 22nd Michigan's November and December 1863 muster rolls listed Clem as "absent without leave [AWOL]." His sister remembered that a wagon dropped him off at the family's front door. "He was wasted to a skeleton," Lizzie commented on her brother's weight. She believed at the time that he weighed no more than sixty pounds.

After being paroled by the Confederates, Sergeant Clem no longer served with the 22nd. By January 1864, he was assigned to the staff of Maj. Gen. George H. Thomas as a mounted orderly. Clem's job was to carry dispatches from Major General Thomas to other officers in the

Army of the Cumberland. Early in Sherman's Atlanta Campaign, Clem was located near Marietta, Georgia, where according to his service record, he was allotted $32.18 for clothing. Sergeant Clem remained near Marietta until June 1864. His job as an orderly was not necessarily a safe one. Messengers were targeted to be killed or captured.

While executing his duties during the Atlanta Campaign, Clem was "nipped in the ear" while handing Gen. John. A. Logan a message, possibly during the Battle of Atlanta, Georgia. During the same battle, Clem's pony was also shot out from under him. Once Atlanta fell, Sgt. John Lincoln Clem was mustered out of service by September 19, 1864. The military had started to muster out of service children younger than sixteen. Officials hoped that these children, once discharged, would return to school. The discharge order came by way of the secretary of war and Special-Order No. 298. John Lincoln Clem, now a civilian, made his way back to his home and family. Lizzie said her brother never "looked more ragged, worn; just skin and bones."

John Lincoln Clem returned home, where he started his schooling again with the goal that he would finally complete high school. He desired to further his military career. When he graduated from Newark High School in 1870, Clem looked for a recommendation for officers' school at West Point. He requested and received an appointment from President Grant, which allowed him to take the military academy entrance exam. In a letter to his brother Louis, Johnny wrote, "I arrived in the city this morning and then went to West Point and spent the day there." He also told his brother in the same letter,

> Do not get homesick. Remember you have a brother who left all friends long before he was as old as you. Go to church tomorrow (every Sunday) and always attend to your Christian duties. Do not miss your school.

His time at West Point did not last long.

> But, alas! For entrance at the Point schooling, rather than military experience, was the prime requisite. I had left school to go to war before

I was ten years old, and my scholarship was sadly in arrears. I failed to pass the examinations.

John Clem appealed to President Grant in person, asking him to either give him a second chance at West Point or to appoint him as an officer. President Grant decided it might be better to appoint Clem a second lieutenant. He received his commission on December 18, 1871. 2nd Lieutenant Clem was attached to the 24th US Infantry. He became a first lieutenant on October 5, 1874, after successfully graduating from artillery school. With his new commission, 1st Lt. John Lincoln Clem was stationed in Texas to fight Native Americans and guard the US/Mexico border. On May 24, 1875, he married Anna Rosetta French, the daughter of Gen. William H. French. Anna gave birth to six children. By 1876, 1st Lieutenant Clem was stationed at Fort McHenry in Maryland when a tragic letter arrived from his family.

In a letter on May 23, 1876, from Fort McHenry, Johnny Clem wrote to his parents and sister Lizzie in response to their message. "I was worried nearly to death when I received your telegram today. I can not believe my dear brother is killed, . . ."

Clem's brother had been killed in an Indian attack near Custer City, South Dakota. Clem was in disbelief because he had just received a letter from Louis. He promised to get to the bottom of it as quickly as he could. General Sherman was contacted for any additional information. "Do not be downhearted, as the Indian reports are false nine times out of ten." Some accounts listed Louis as dying in the battle of the Little Bighorn. However, his name does not appear in the lists of those killed. He was not a soldier but believed to be a civilian accompanying a scouting party.

John Clem continued in the same letter, "I will telegraph you if I hear good news, which I hope to God I will hear tomorrow." Johnny Clem did not get the good news he so hoped to transmit to his family. He had tried his best to steer his brother away from the adventure that his older brother craved. In a prior letter, John had told his younger brother not to head out west for adventure, explaining to Louis that it would better to learn from his older brother's mistakes and remain in school. He worked to secure a job for Louis in the Pension Bureau in Washington, DC.

But like his older brother, Louis craved adventure more than schooling. He left his job to head west, never to be seen by his older brother again. Johnny put himself in charge of bringing his brother's body back east to its final resting place in Mt. Calvary Cemetery. Louis Klem was just twenty-one years old.

1st Lt. John Clem's military career continued to grow. In May 1882, he was commissioned captain and commissioned quartermaster. By 1901, he again was elevated in rank to a major, as well as quartermaster. Finally, yet another commission raised his rank to colonel and an assistant quartermaster. His time in war was not done; he would also serve during the Spanish-American War in 1898. If these were times for career advancement, they were intermingled with tragedy. His wife Anna died in 1899, leaving John Clem to raise his fourteen-year-old son John Jr. Roughly two years later, Clem remarried. Her name was Mary Elizabeth "Bessie" Sullivan, with whom he would have a daughter named Anne Elizabeth, born in 1906.

Clem's military career was coming to an end as he reached the army's mandatory retirement age. In 1910 according to the US Federal Census, Clem was living with his wife and young daughter at Fort Sam Houston. Five years later, on August 13, 1915, he became a brigadier general, and finally, his last commission when he was already retired was promotion to major general. His residence was in Washington, DC, and Clem had been part of the Quartermasters Department since the 1880s, helping supply the army.

Even though retired, Maj. Gen. John Lincoln Clem remained active in military affairs. He continued to be a celebrity, frequently attending Civil War veterans' gatherings, including Memorial Day wreath-laying ceremonies. The Drummer Boy of Chickamauga offered his services in 1918 when the United States entered World War I. Major General Clem offered to come out of retirement and offered his services personally to President Woodrow Wilson. He looked forward to a "return to active duty." President Wilson declined Clem's offer because of the retired major general's advanced age.

Although Clem became a permanent fixture in Washington, DC, after his retirement, he eventually moved to San Antonio, Texas, in 1935, for health reasons. The retired army officer lived in San Antonio until his death on May 13, 1937. While getting ready for bed at 9:45 p.m., he was stricken with what the attending physician listed as "dilatation of heart-sudden death." Senility was recorded as an indirect cause of death. Eight decades after he had stowed away with the 22nd Michigan Infantry at age ten, Clem was buried with honors in Arlington National Cemetery on May 18, 1937, where he was interred in Section 2 Grave no. 933, in the shadow of Robert E. Lee's Arlington mansion.

Chapter Two

Susie King Taylor (Nurse and Teacher)

Nurse, teacher, and author Susie Taylor has often been overlooked in Civil War studies, though she was the only African-American woman to write her memoirs and publish them after the Civil War. Her memoirs chronicle her time that she served, without pay, during the Civil War. A determined thirteen-year-old freed slave, she nursed the freed African-American Union regiment the 1st South Carolina. Later this regiment was renamed the 33rd United States Colored Infantry Regiment.

Susie Baker Taylor was born a slave on the Valentine Grest Plantation on Midway (Isle of Wright), Georgia, in Liberty County on August 6, 1848. She was the first of six children born to Hagar Ann and Raymond Baker, married in 1847, but only Susie, a younger brother, and younger sister survived. Slave marriages were not recognized by law. If slaves were allowed the legal protection of marriage, it would make it difficult for their owners to sell them. Many times, slave couples lived on different plantations. Families could and were often broken apart at the will of their respective masters. This was the case with Raymond and Hagar, and Susie's family was broken up while she was young.

The Grest family did not have children of their own. Valentin Grest, the owner of the plantation, often traveled for long periods. He left his wife Frederica alone to supervise their plantation and its thirty slaves. In 1860, slaves in bondage on the plantation ranged in ages from one to sixty. Lacking company or children, she took an interest in Susie and her younger brother.

Susie Baker Taylor

Susie's maternal grandmother Dolly Reed lived in Savannah, Georgia, and kept in touch with her last surviving child, Hagar Ann. It is believed that Dolly was a semi-free African American. Savannah was about forty miles from the Grest Plantation. According to historian Catherine Clinton in her article, "I Gave My Services Willingly," "she lived out-paying her own keep and giving her owner the rest of her earnings." It was Dolly who requested Susie and her brother come live with her in Savannah.

In 1856, when Mr. Grest was approached with the idea of sending Susie and her brother to live with Dolly, he agreed. Susie's life dramatically changed. Frederica Grest had started to teach Susie and her brother how to read, which was considered illegal. Once with their grandmother, Susie and her brother continued their educations. Susie recalled that Dolly sent her to the home of a Mrs. Mary Woodhouse who, along with her daughter, taught classes clandestinely out of their home. This was considered dangerous because the punishment for a person of color teaching another person of color to read or write in the state of Georgia during this time was a severe whipping, a fine, or in some cases, both.

Susie remembered in an often-quoted passage from her autobiography, "we went every day about nine o'clock with our books wrapped in paper to prevent the police or white persons from seeing them." They learned in a large class with other children. Sometimes the class was as large as thirty-five students. "I remained at her school for two years or more." After she had learned all that Ms. Woodhouse could teach her, Susie left for another clandestine school in the house of Mrs. Mary Beasley. Susie and her brother "continued until May 1860. . . ." Once again, Mrs. Beasley taught Susie all she knew. Her grandmother looked for someone else to continue teaching her granddaughter.

Katie O'Connor, a childhood friend of Susie's, lived "on the next corner of the street from my house, and who attended a convent." Susie approached Katie to continue her covert education. Katie agreed to teach Susie if she promised not to tell a soul, especially Katie's father, what they were doing. Eventually, Katie entered the convent full-time, and Susie's education once again came to a temporary end. Dolly Reed looked again to find a more permanent teacher for her grandchildren. Dolly found out that her landlord had a fifteen-year-old son named James Blouis. James attended a local high school. When Reed approached him to instruct Susie, he agreed—the only stipulation, as always, if she kept the class secret. This time Susie's education with James would be cut short by the start of the Civil War. Both James and his older brother Eugene, who had graduated from St. Mary's College in Maryland, joined the Savannah Volunteer Guards in May 1861, shortly after the attack on Fort Sumter in South Carolina's Charleston Harbor.

The Civil War came early to Savannah in April 1862. Susie remembered that "Union soldiers were firing on Fort Pulaski; I was sent out into the country to my mother." This was known as the Siege of Fort Pulaski, which occurred on April 10 and 11, 1862. Union major general William Tecumseh Sherman blockaded the port of Savannah. When Fort Pulaski finally capitulated on April 11, Grest instructed Susie to move farther inland to the Grest property, quite possibly not wanting his slave to fall into the hands of the Union as contraband. Seeing a chance at freedom, Susie made her move during the chaos of war.

Susie eventually fled the Grest Plantation with her uncle and his family to St. Catherine's Island, an island off the coast of Georgia roughly ten miles long and three miles wide. They would remain on the island until late in April 1862 when Susie boarded the Union gunboat USS *Potomska* bound for St. Simons Island. The island was a strategic one because it was halfway between Savannah and Jacksonville, Florida. Robert E. Lee had evacuated the island of St. Simons. He hoped to use the islands for supplies, as a base of operations, to subvert the Union blockade of Georgia. The Union occupied the island for the rest of the war.

Fate took a turn while Susie was a passenger on the boat taking her and others to St. Simons Island. Captain Whitmore, commanding the gunboat, asked Susie where she was from and if she could read and write. Susie replied that before the war started, she lived in Savannah. As far as reading and writing, Susie was able to do both. Captain Whitmore, for some reason, suspected that she might be lying to him. Captain Whitmore asked her to prove her abilities to him, which she successfully did. Once satisfied, he asked Susie if, while on St. Simons, Susie would agree to teach freed African Americans how to read and write in a school located at Gaston Bluff. Susie recalled that once the school was up and running, she educated as many as forty students during the day. When the sun set, she convened school for the adults.

In June 1862, the war came close to Susie's school. There was a skirmish between Confederate soldiers and soldiers from the Union army's 1st South Carolina Volunteers coming from Hope Place. Additional soldiers were sent to reinforce the troops already involved in the fight. They were successful in not only repelling the Confederates but captured the boat they used to come to St. Simons. Although they scoured the area for the Confederate soldiers, they had absconded and taken shelter in the home of an elderly slave by the name of Henry Capers. Henry gave the attackers a boat in which to make their escape to the safety of their lines.

Susie continued in her capacity as a teacher. This role came to an end in October 1862, when some troops left the island. They boarded the *Ben-De-Ford* bound for Beaufort, South Carolina. It was while on St. Simons Island that Susie met her future husband, Sgt. Edward King, a freed noncommissioned officer in the Union army. Sergeant King was from Darien, Georgia. He had enlisted in Company E of the 1st South Carolina.

When they arrived at Camp Saxton in South Carolina, the African-American soldiers still had not been paid for their service. Without pay, these soldiers could not support their families. It forced women like Susie and other women to become laundresses for white officers to support their families. The issue of pay would come to a head in the not too distant future.

Shortly after arriving at Camp Saxton, the 1st South Carolina and the 48th New York started an expedition on the Doboy River in Georgia. The steamer *Darlington*, the *Ben-De-Ford*, and the gunboat *Madgie* served as transports for supplies, men, and protection. During that expedition, the Union forces destroyed the Confederates' valuable salt works, an essential commodity in a pre-refrigerator society for preserving food. In addition to destroying the salt stores, the soldiers secured valuable lumber and sundry supplies from Confederate camps along the river.

Here the 1st South Carolina Volunteers stayed until January 1863. While there, Susie was employed as a laundress. While on the expedition,

Susie would have heard of Lincoln's Emancipation Proclamation at a service held just for that purpose. Dr. W. H. Brisbane read the proclamation, and afterward, the regiment was given its regimental colors. "It was a glorious day for us all, and we enjoyed every minute of it . . . ," Susie remembered.

The Second Confiscation Militia Act of July 17, 1862, had prohibited African Americans from being involved in combat; they had mainly been used for manual labor. The Emancipation Proclamation was an essential milestone because it allowed newly freed African Americans to serve in a combat role. Lincoln stated in the proclamation, "And I further declare and make known, that such persons of suitable condition, will be received into the armed service of the United States to garrison forts, positions, stations, and other places, and to man vessels of all sorts in said service."

Later, in her memoir, Susie wrote that "the first suits worn by the boys were red coats and pants, which they disliked very much, for they said, 'the rebels see us, miles away.'" During this time, the "colored" troops had not been paid for a year and a half. To bring in money, members of the soldiers' families continued to wash officers' laundry and sell baked goods, which brought in extra cash. When the federal government decided to grant the troops half-pay, the soldiers felt disgraced. Pvt. Sylvester Ray of the 2nd US Colored Cavalry summed it up in June 1864, while standing trial for not accepting half-pay, "none of us will sign again for seven dollars a month. . . ." Private Ray stood trial because he refused to accept the $7 which was less than whites received for the same job.

On January 23, 1863, the regiment moved up St. Mary's River to capture Confederate stores and, in the words of the commanding officer of the 1st South Carolina, T. W. Higginson, to carry, "the regimental flag and President's proclamation far into the interior of Georgia and Florida." It was at Township, Florida, that the 1st South Carolina fought a small battle after being surprised by a Confederate cavalry company. Although able to repel the attackers, they took eight casualties. Because nighttime was fast approaching, they thought it was not wise to pursue the Confederate attackers.

Almost the entire forty miles of St. Mary's River was rife with skirmishes between Confederates onshore and the Union soldiers ascending the river. When they finally returned to camp, the 1st South Carolina had still managed to secure valuable supplies from the Confederates along the river, including bricks, railroad iron, and more timber. The Union army badly needed these supplies for construction purposes. During these raids, copious amounts of food supplies were taken, such as rice and live-stock. Colonel Higginson, a noted abolitionist, took pride in confiscating from a slave jail "three sets of stocks, of different structure, the chains and staples used for confining prisoners to the door, and the key to the building. They furnish good illustrations of the infernal barbarism against which we contend." What made the expedition a success, he felt, was Corp. Robert Sutton, "of Company G, formerly a slave upon the Saint Mary's River." Sutton knew the entire stretch of the river very well and guided the expedition safely up the river.

Although hired as a laundress, Susie states that she was not paid for a few years in her autobiography. Susie became a jack-of-all-trades to survive. Although she thought of herself primarily as a teacher, nurses were sorely needed. Variola or smallpox was starting to make soldiers sick in camp in February 1863. There were several cases. Some soldiers died because they had not been inoculated. Many doctors, nurses, and soldiers were nervous about attending to these sick individuals. Susie felt the men needed her, and she saw it as her duty to nurse them. "I was not in the least afraid of the small-pox. I had been vaccinated, and I drank sassafras tea constantly, which kept my blood purged and prevented me from contracting this dreaded scourge. . . ."

According to Brigadier-General of Volunteers Rufus Saxton's report, the 1st South Carolina started operations against Jacksonville, Florida, on March 6, 1863. It was a joint operation with elements of the 2nd South Carolina Volunteers, commanded by Colonel T. W. Higginson. They were successful in capturing Jacksonville on March 10, 1863. Susie writes that a skirmish on March 11, was a "lively fight which lasted sev-eral hours, and our boys were nearly captured by the Confederates. . . ." In the end they managed to drive back the Rebels. The South Carolina Volunteers occupied Jacksonville from March 10 to March 31, 1863.

While the soldiers were on their latest campaign in Jacksonville, Susie did not do a lot of laundry but instead started teaching again. "I taught a great many of the comrades in Company E to read and write, when they were off duty." Her husband, who was also educated, sometimes taught with his wife. When not teaching, "I was glad, however, to be allowed to go with the regiment, to care for the sick and afflicted comrades."

While in camp, Susie added yet another duty to the others she had learned since St. Catherine's Island early in the war. Always trying to make herself as useful as possible, Susie did some soldiering by helping with cleaning rifled muskets, which had to be cleaned regularly to keep them in good working order. Black powder gummed up the mechanisms, including the barrel. Part of her duties was also checking the integrity of the cartridges. The cartridges were wrapped in paper, which protected the powder; if they become damp or wet, it could result in a musket that did not fire. After cleaning the muskets, she charged or reloaded the musket for use. Susie understood the importance of this task: "her men's" lives depended on her.

According to historian Catherine Clinton, Susie "[became] a skilled apprentice to Union surgeons switching from washing bandages to applying them." When she was not following the regiments on their expeditions, she frequently went to Beaufort, South Carolina, to visit the hospital set up for "colored" troops. While touring the hospital during the first week of April 1863, she met Clara Barton, future founder of the American Red Cross. Dr. Stephen B. Oates, in his book on the life of Clara Barton, *A Woman of Valor*, writes that possibly Dr. Ruggers suggested that Barton visit "General Hospital Number 10 for Colored Troops." The two women toured the hospital together. In her writings, Susie stated, "I honored her for her devotion and care of these men."

On July 9-10, 1863, the 1st South Carolina were on yet another expedition, this time on the South Edisto River aboard the steamer *John Adams*, the transport *Enoch Dean*, and the small tug *Governor Milton*. The purpose of this expedition was to destroy a bridge that spanned the Charleston and Savannah Roads. The force was composed of some 250 officers and men of the regiment, "and a section of the 1st Connecticut Battery. . . ." They engaged the Confederates at Willstown, and "engaged a three-gun field battery there stationed." Willstown Bluff was located on the part of the Edisto once known as the Pon-Pon River.

After an exchange, the Confederate battery retreated, which opened up a landing of thirty men under the command of Lt. James B. West. The vessels had some problems with how shallow the river could be in spots, and some of the ships ran aground, including the *Governor Milton*. When the Milton ran aground again when descending the Edisto, the *John Adams* came to the *Milton*'s rescue but could not dislodge it. The decision was made to abandon the ship, which was now coming under heavy fire from the bluff near Willstown. They decided to burn their own vessel, but the haul from the expedition was still a good one that included freed African Americans, cotton, and numerous Confederate prisoners. Unfortunately, during this last battle on the Edisto, Col. T. W. Higginson was wounded.

Toward the end of November 1863, Companies E and K were sent to Pocatalico, South Carolina, to neutralize a Confederate battery. A skirmish ensued with Rebel cavalry near Cunningham's Bluff on November 24. It almost ended badly for the two companies when they were engaged by Confederate cavalry, but they were able to turn the tide on the attackers and, in the process, secure some prisoners. Sergeant King, Susie's husband, fell over an embankment, severely injuring his hip, and she spent most of her time nursing her husband's wound.

In February 1864, the 1st South Carolina was reorganized. They would become the 33rd US Colored Troops. The 33rd was incorporated into the Department of the South. As the 33rd they were part of operations against Charleston, South Carolina, when they were ordered to Folly Island, a barrier island of about seven square miles that was used to stage attacks on Charleston. In her memoirs, Susie described Folly Island as a spit of land with not much on or growing on it. By the end of June, they were told to prepare to move to Morris Island in Charlestown Harbor, which they occupied by July 1, 1864.

Periodically, the 33rd was shelled by Confederate batteries from nearby Fort Gregg, located on the tip of Morris Island at Cummings Point. This fort helped protect Fort Sumter and also Charlestown, South Carolina. It was decided that Fort Gregg needed to be attacked.

In July 1864, with the 103rd New York, they reached Pawnell Landing in the dark. While the men were on their journey to Fort Gregg, all

Susie and her friend Mary Shaw could do was wait anxiously in camp. They grew sleepy and finally decided to retire to the tent they shared. "We went back to bed, but not to sleep, for the fleas nearly ate us alive." They sat up the remainder of the night when by daybreak, the wounded started arriving on July 2, 1864. She wrote that Samuel Anderson was the first member of the company to arrive. Others followed, "some with their legs off, arm gone, foot off, and wounds of all kinds imaginable." She learned that the troops were discovered as they waded through creeks and marshes. The wounds and suffering were worse for the 103rd. She worked feverously to alleviate their sufferings.

> *I asked the doctor at the hospital what I could get for them to eat. They wanted soup, but that I could not get; but I had a few cans of condensed milk and some turtle eggs, so I thought I would try to make some custard . . . This I carried to the men, who enjoyed it very much.*

The next month, August, the 33rd were ordered to Cole Island until October. In November, Susie almost lost her life.

On November 1, 1864, six companies were detailed to go to Gregg Landing, Port Royal Ferry. The Confederates discovered them, and a stalemate ensued between the two opposing armies. An officer told Susie they needed to abandon the island to get on one of the transports to safety. However, the soldiers were able to beat back the Confederates.

All around Susie King was death and destruction. There is no doubt it took its toll on the now seventeen-year-old. She had some close calls, but not one like on November 23, 1864, when she secured a pass to go from Hilton Head to Beaufort by way of a "yacht." Susie almost died when the vessel capsized.

> *I remember going down twice. As I rose the second time, I caught hold of the sail and managed to hold fast to some part of the boat, and we drifted and shouted as loud as we could, trying to attract the attention of some of the government boats which were going up and down the river. . . .*

When they were about to give up finally, they were heard on Ladies' Island. Susie and some of the other survivors were picked up by government boats. They were in the water for some four hours. Susie was very ill from all the water she took into her lungs and stomach. In January 1865, she would return to Cole Island to be attended to by a Doctor Miner. She recovered but had a lingering cough for a long time.

In February 1865, much to Susie's dismay, after the capitulation of Charleston, South Carolina, the retreating Confederate forces set fire to the city as the Union landed in the town from Cole Island. The Union forces helped the citizens put out the fires raging throughout the city. Susie was given quarters on South Battery Street, "Where I assisted in caring for the sick and injured comrades." The soldiers were camped out at the racetrack until March 12, 1865, when they were sent to Savannah, Georgia. They arrived on March 13, 1865. They remained there for just over a week and were detailed to Augusta, Georgia. The soldiers stayed in Augusta for a month, until the war came to an end in April 1865. The 33rd then went to Hamburg, South Carolina, and finally back to Charleston by November 1865. In January, Susie wrote that they had returned to Morris Island. Finally, "they mustered out of service on February 9, 1866 at Fort Wagner, above the graves of Colonel Robert Gould Shaw and the men of the 54th Massachusetts."

After the war, Susie settled in Savannah, Georgia, with her husband. While in Savannah, she continued her life as an educator. She taught recently freed African Americans, both children and adults. Susie recounted that her husband "was a boss carpenter, but being just mustered out of the army, and the prejudice against his race being still too strong to insure him much work at his trade, he took contracts for unloading vessels. . . ." While working on the piers, he died on September 16, 1866, leaving a wife who was about to give birth to their first child.

Teaching became more difficult for Susie King when her paying students began leaving for the free schools that had started opening up across the country. Susie left Savannah and journeyed to Liberty County, Georgia, where she taught there for a year. However, she did not like "country life."

By 1868, she left her young child with her mother, Hagar, and decided to become a domestic servant for a local family. She could not earn a living as a teacher anymore. Susie lived there for quite a while, but she changed occupations again after finding the work too hard. What helped her during these difficult times was that she was granted her late husband's bounty of $100. She put this money in the bank while she worked for Mrs. Charlie Green as a laundress. Still wanting a better life and possibly a better climate than the war-torn South, she headed north. Susie arrived in Boston, Massachusetts, in 1874; in 1879, she met her second husband, Russell L. Taylor, originally from Georgia. After she remarried in 1879, she had started working for the Smith family on Walnut Avenue in the Boston Highlands. When Mrs. Smith died, Russell was listed in a census as a shoreman at the Boston docks.

The following year, Susie and her husband almost died in a steamer accident, the second boating mishap for Susie. On the foggy night of June 11, 1880, they were on the steamer *Stonington* on their way to New York City. Another vessel, the *Narragansett*, collided with the *Stonington*. She heard "the passengers shrieking, groaning, running about, leaping into the water," from the *Narragansett*, which was in flames. Lifeboats saved many from both boats. Remarkably, they resumed their trip, arriving in Manhattan by 9:30 p.m. According to the *New York Times*, thirty people died in the collision.

While living in Massachusetts, Susie continued making her living as a servant for wealthy white families in Boston. One such family was the Gray family, who lived on Beacon Street. Susie continued to take pride in the role that she played during the Civil War. She also wanted to honor the soldiers who gave of themselves so bravely. In 1886, she founded the Corps 67, Women's Relief Corps, which was an auxiliary to the Grand Army of the Republic. Susie was quite active, starting as a guard, then secretary, treasurer, and finally, in 1893, the organization's president. Three years later, she helped complete a roster of the Union veterans of the War of the Rebellion now residing in Massachusetts.

Susie King Taylor did on occasion return to the South. This included seeing her grandmother for what ended up being the last time. She also returned in the 1890s for the death of her son. Susie had left her son with her mother shortly after his birth. According to the 1900 US Federal Census, Susie and her husband lived on 34 Buckingham Street in Boston with their niece. Russell died on October 11, 1901. The death record states that he died of Bright's disease, a form of kidney disease related to hypertension and heart disease. His occupation the year he died was a laborer.

In 1901, Susie started writing her memoirs about her experiences during the Civil War with the 33rd US Colored Infantry. In the introduction to her book, published in 1902, she states, "I wrote to Colonel C. T. Trowbridge (who had command of this regiment), asking his opinion and advice on the matter. His answer to me was, 'Go ahead! Write it; that is just what I should do, were I in your place, and I will give you all the assistance you may need, whenever you require it.' This inspired me very much." By 1910, she was listed as a servant and lived on South Huntington Avenue in Boston. However, she worked as a servant not in a home but a hospital.

Susie Taylor's health was starting to decline by the time of the 1910 census. She suffered from chronic nephritis, an inflammation of the kidneys. Two days before her death on October 7, 1912, she had episodes of syncope or fainting. She was buried in Mount Hope Cemetery in Roslindale, Massachusetts, alongside her second husband in an unmarked grave.

The state of Georgia only recently recognized the achievements of this remarkable African American by erecting a historic marker in the Midway First Presbyterian Church cemetery. The Georgia Historical Society, Waters Foundation, Inc., and the Susie King Taylor Women's Institute & Ecology Center erected it in her honor. In 2019 a ceremony was held where it is believed her remains were interred for a new stone's dedication.

CHAPTER THREE

Charles Whipple Hadley
(Bravery at Shiloh)

CHARLES WHIPPLE HADLEY WAS BORN ON FEBRUARY 11, 1844, THE SON of Rufus S. and Sarah Ann (Jones) Hadley. In the 1860 Federal Census, his father was an attorney with a real estate value of $4,700 and a personal estate of $2,500, making his family well off for the time. Sarah owned real estate totaling $800 and a personal estate of $400. Charles was the oldest of seven children. The family had migrated from New Hampshire west to Anamosa, Iowa, before 1860.

When Charles entered college in 1860, the nation had grown tired of compromise over the issue of slavery. In 1846 when the war had started with Mexico, Senator David Wilmot of Pennsylvania had proposed that all lands acquired from Mexico would be free states. This became known as the Wilmot Proviso. Senator Wilmot's plan much angered the South's planters, who owned the majority of slaves in the South. His plan did not pass Congress, but the voice of abolition was growing. Charles Whipple Hadley would have grown up aware of the debates over the future of slavery. His family was against slavery.

War was averted again with the Compromise of 1850, which contained a clause known as the Fugitive Slave Act. It made harboring runaway slaves a crime. The Compromise of 1850 overturned the Missouri Compromise. It was followed by the Kansas-Nebraska Act, proposed by future presidential candidate Senator Stephen A. Douglas, which allowed for popular sovereignty. It passed in 1854. States coming into the Union

Charles Whipple Hadley

west of Iowa voted on whether they wanted to permit slavery or not. This led to large-scale violence in both Kansas and Nebraska between pro-slavery and antislavery factions.

The last presidential election before the start of the Civil War was the 1856 election. It was between Democrat James Buchanan, Whig John C. Fremont, and Republican Millard Fillmore. Buchanan became the last president before the Civil War. He tried to keep the nation together as the country continued to move toward war with the 1857 Dred Scott decision and Northern support for John Brown's Harper's Ferry raid in 1859.

Charles Whipple Hadley started college at age sixteen in the presidential election year of 1860, a year in which the South was threatening secession if Abraham Lincoln became the next president of the United States. While at Cornell College in Mount Vernon, Iowa, he lodged in "the house of a Mr. Spangler." While there, he joined the local Republican Club, which was a relatively new party, running its presidential candidate, Abraham Lincoln. Hadley, becoming energized by the election, went to a political gathering and afterward, he recorded his views on the election. Hadley had gone to see the Democratic nominee for president, US senator Stephen A. Douglas from Illinois. He observed that "More Republicans went to hear a Democrat speak than Democrats." Hadley also recorded who he believed should be the winner of the election even though he could not vote, writing in his diary, "Hurrah for Lincoln and Hamlin." Hannibal Hamlin, a US senator from Maine, would become Lincoln's vice president.

When it became clear that Lincoln would be victorious, South Carolina voted to secede from the Union on December 20, 1860, the first Southern state to do so. They would be followed by Texas, Louisiana, Mississippi, Alabama, Florida, and Georgia. This left Virginia, North Carolina, Kentucky, Tennessee, Missouri, Delaware, Maryland, and Arkansas, which were also slave states. Charles Whipple Hadley, still in college, probably learned of Lincoln's First Inaugural Address: "In your hands, my dissatisfied fellow countrymen, and not in mine, is the momentous issue of *civil war*. The Government will not assail you. You can have no conflict without being yourselves the aggressors. . . ." The South fired the first shot of the war on April 12, 1861. Fort Sumter, located in Charlestown Harbor, capitulated three days later. Four more slave states would join what became known as the Confederate States of America: Virginia, Arkansas, Tennessee, and North Carolina.

When word reached Charles Whipple Hadley of the attack on Sumter, according to Ora Williams in *College Student and Soldier Boy*, Charles had become a teacher at a local school to help pay for his schooling. "South Carolina has withdrawn from the Union," Hadley recorded in his daily diary. "[O]ther states are threatening to do the same. Let'em went."

When President Lincoln called for three hundred thousand men for the Union army, Hadley decided to volunteer. "I enlisted today in the Union Army for 3 years." E. L. Warner raised a company of men, including Hadley, who was taken into the army as a 4th corporal. During his time in the Union army, he would leave Anamosa and march to Davenport, Iowa, on November 6, 1861. The same day, with neighbors and friends who enlisted simultaneously, he was "sworn into the U.S. Service." He would be a part of the 14th Iowa Regiment Company H. With this company, he would be in some of the momentous battles of the Civil War, including Fort Donelson, Shiloh, and the Siege of Vicksburg. His pay, he recorded, was "$13.00 per month."

After marching to Davenport, Company H remained there at Camp McClellan until November 29, 1861. "We are all impatient to leave." However, the regiment was delayed. By 5:00 a.m. they were in "Jollyett, Ill." They traveled all night. "We reached this place about four o'clock this morning." They boarded the Illinois Central Railroad, "half starved to death." Eventually boarding the steamboat *Meteor*, "on board of which we stayed all night, starting at 6 in the morning we reached St. Louis about 8 o'clock a.m." They were "quartered in Benton Barracks." By December 6, 1861, Hadley was given a pass to go to St. Louis. "I got a dish of oisters [*sic*] for dinner (.25) at a saloon. I also bought a flute (1.50) & book (.50)."

Benton Barracks was "originally a privately owned facility, used by the St. Louis Agricultural and Mechanical Association." It was used by the western part of the Union army to train the recruits such as Hadley. It was still relatively new when Hadley arrived. It had been created in August 1861 under the direction of Maj. Gen. John C. Fremont. By the time Hadley arrived, Major-General Fremont was relieved of command by Lincoln and replaced by Brig. Gen. William Tecumseh Sherman.

Military camps with so many people in one area became rife with disease. Sanitation was nonexistent in many cases. Clean drinking water and quality food were hard to find in many situations, becoming a chief complaint of the soldiers. Camps were compromised by typhus, small-pox, dysentery, and other diseases. A large number of men succumbed to disease rather than combat. On December 9, 1861, Corporal Hadley recorded that "I am quite sick this morning. I was taken with a very severe sick headache yesterday about noon. . . ." When he went to the regimental doctor, he was told he had a high fever. After a brief period of feeling better, he was again taken ill on December 18, the same day he records, "our news this morning was that New Orleans was taken & that we had whiped [sic] them twice in Kentucky." Possibly he was ill because he had been vaccinated against smallpox.

The scourge of an army, smallpox was rampant in the 14th Iowa. About the same time smallpox was making an appearance, measles, which today we do not think of as a deadly sickness, took the life of Had-ley's friend Fred Haymaker. It, too, was making many of the men sick at Benton Barracks. During Christmas 1861, Corporal Hadley reported in his diary that he still felt ill.

Hadley was anxious for many reasons about leaving St. Louis. After other trips, including to Paducah, Kentucky, by February 8, 1862, his company was at Fort Henry, Tennessee, taken earlier by the Union. Company H was ordered on February 11 from Fort Henry 12 miles west to Fort Donelson, where they arrived on February 13, 1862. When they were two miles from the fort, they heard the roar of thunderous cannon that shook the ground. Hadley recorded they "expect to see some fight." We do not know if he was excited or fearing the engagement. Hadley wrote that the men were so tired from days of marching that the men slept soundly before nearing the fort. As they were pushed into battle, Hadley could only be described as horrified as he later recorded that when he was within "6 rods of the works O'Neil just shot in the head Sargent a few feet from me just shot."

By February 17, Hadley and Company H occupied the inner fort and were readying to attack the works. Hadley recorded that "we received a storm of bullets." A soldier next to him was "cut across the temple & with the exclamation oh murder I'm shot he rolled over & was taken off." During this battle, Hadley was one of the color guards. He was charged with carrying the regimental colors. It was considered a disgrace if they were allowed to be captured by the enemy or allowed to fall, and men carrying the regimental colors were favorite targets of sharpshooters. "One of the color guards of which I am one was shot through the head within two feet of me spattering the blood on my left arm and face." Hadley himself had a close call when "a bullet went through his cartridge box," nearly missing his body when it exited. He would not be at the raising of the white flag, signaling the surrender of Fort Donelson. Hadley was removed from the field with what he described as a "severe attack of the rheumatism." He was sent to the hospital to recover.

Significantly recovered, though not in top shape, Hadley left Fort Donelson for Savannah, Tennessee, on March 7th, arriving there on March 17th. From there, his company made its way to Pittsburg Landing, which was located thirteen miles above Savannah, Tennessee. He jotted down that the Rebels were about twenty miles from them. Company H of the 14th Iowa had their tents pitched about one mile from the Tennessee River. What would become the fight of his lifetime was beginning to take shape. The battle would forever become known in the North for the small church not far from where Hadley was camped. The church was called Shiloh, a name taken from the Bible, which ironically meant "peace."

The Battle of Shiloh or Pittsburg Landing was part of Maj. Gen. Ulysses S. Grant's Western Campaign. He had successfully subdued both the Tennessee and Cumberland Rivers with the surrender of Forts Donelson and Henry. These rivers allowed the Union to ship vital supplies. It also gave the Union control of Kentucky and much of Tennessee. After the two forts' surrender, Grant was able to focus his sights on Corinth in northern Mississippi.

The Confederates under Brig. Gen. Albert Sidney Johnston and General P. G. T. Beauregard decided to defend Corinth's vital railroad link. Here, Johnston hoped to regroup his army of about forty-five thousand. Major General Grant hoped to combine forces with Maj. Gen. Don Carlos Buell to attack Corinth. Grant's troops arrived at Pittsburg Landing in March 1862. In her book *The Shadow of Shiloh*, Gail Stephens explains that there would be "five divisions at Pittsburg Landing, Tennessee, and a sixth at Crump's Landing, four miles from Grant's headquarters, in Savannah, Tennessee." Grant waited for Buell's army to join him, which would swell his ranks to over sixty thousand.

General Johnston knew that Grant was waiting for General Buell's reinforcements. Instead of waiting for this, Johnston decided to fight the Union encamped along the Tennessee River. This attack took place on the morning of April 6, 1862. Since many of the Union troops were still considered "green," the Union defenses broke quickly. The Confederate army pushed the Union lines almost to the banks of the Tennessee River. Some Union lines held, especially where Charles Whipple Hadley was located with the 14th Iowa. He was dug in along a sunken road on the land of J. R. Duncan, which formed the Hornet's Nest (a name given later because of the whizzing of the bullets that to its defenders and attackers sounded like angry hornets).

Hadley and other soldiers in the Hornet's Nest were successfully able to hold off the Rebel charge, allowing the soldiers who were retreating to regroup in the rear. Finally, it gave the troops time for General Buell's army to arrive. What also helped the Union was that a Minié ball had clipped an artery in Johnston's leg. He quickly bled out, leaving command to Beauregard. After several attacks by the Confederates on the Hornet's Nest, the Confederate command realized that the only way to overcome its entrenched defenders was with artillery assistance. Confederate brigadier general Daniel Ruggles used over sixty artillery guns to blast the men along the sunken road.

Charles Hadley recorded the carnage and the helplessness of the situation in his diary. "We laid on the ground gained until about 9 o'clock when the enemy gained ground rapidly on our left flank we commenced falling back as the enemy came up the 14th Iowa covered the retreat about face & held them at bay for 15 minutes amid a perfect storm of ball & shell the 14th suffered terribly seeing that we were nearly cut off we fell back rapidly in the retreat we lost many we drew up at the camp of the 3d Iowa here we were entirely surrounded & had to surrender. . . ." Hadley, along with most of the surviving Union soldiers in the Hornet's Nest, which included Maj. Gen. Benjamin Prentiss, were taken prisoners. Hadley wrote in his diary that he almost got away but was "captured at 6:05 P.M." losses on both sides were staggering, with Shiloh recording the highest number of casualties of any Civil War battle up to that time. Gettysburg would later eclipse Shiloh.

"The place we were marched to after being captured, camped on a cornfield & laid in mud rained all night." A prisoner of war at Centre Hill, Tennessee, on April 7, Hadley was unsure of his fate or where he would be marched to during the coming days. He would march from Centre Hill to Corinth. They arrived at Corinth on the night of the 7th. He believed it was a twenty-mile march. Once there, the prisoners were loaded into railroad cars "during a heavy rain storm." Hadley estimated the number of captured at about twelve thousand. By way of rumor, he heard they were to be transported to "Tuscalacy [*sic*], Alabama." There were forty men in each car, where each man was given "two hard crackers & a little piece of meat." They were to stop in Jackson, Mississippi, where crowds slowed the train as people came out to see what a "live" Yankee looked like. They spent two days in Jackson housed in a "large cotton warehouse."

By April 17th, Hadley arrived in Mobile, Alabama. He felt that the prisoners were being taken care of and looked after well by the Confederates in charge. Late in April, the men were on the move again; this time, they were loaded on a boat for Cahaba, Alabama. The prisoners were to be housed in an unfinished warehouse on the banks of the Alabama River. Feeling bad for the prisoners, "the ladies of the town sent in a beautiful supply of cornbread & meat. We shall long remember our breakfast, for we were hungry as dogs the boys are all in good spirits. . . ." What partially kept up their spirits was the periodic rumors and newspapers confirming that the Union was making great strides against the Confederacy. If they liked where they were being housed, it would not last long. Once again, they would be on the move.

Guards ordered Hadley and the other prisoners with him to cook up enough rations for a journey. Perhaps tiring of their situation and wanting to be home gave rise to rumors of possible parole back to the North. This was not to be at this time. Instead, they were being ferried to another camp by way of the ship the *St. Charles*. On May 3, 1862, they arrived in Montgomery at sundown, where they were forced to march to their next quarters. Their latest shelter was an amphitheater in an old fairground. "It is an old one no seats remain it is fast going to ruin. . . ." After a brief rest, the prisoners were roused to continue the end of their journey, Camp Oglethorpe, in Georgia, which was also an old fairground. "It is a large level piece of ground half shaded by pine trees we are just turned loose in here with guards stationed around the outside . . . ." Camp Oglethorpe was located along the Ocmulgee River, in Macon, Georgia.

While at Camp Oglethorpe, the prisoners talked of missing home, played an early form of baseball called "ball," checkers, or marbles. The commander he recorded was Major Hardee, who was a nephew of the Confederate General Hardee. He agreed with how Major Hardee was treating them. There was joy as newspapers told of the Union army making gains against the Confederates. A local newspaper despaired over the destruction of the gunboat *Merrimack*, originally a Union boat that had been rebuilt into an ironclad by the Confederates, in an epic battle between the *Monitor* and *Merrimack* on March 9, 1862, off Virginia's coast.

Camp Oglethorpe started to change for the prisoners in mid-May 1862. Hadley wrote that he was not feeling well. Also, soldiers around him began to become sick with various illnesses. His diary begins recording the men's names who died in the camp. Some he noted were from other regiments and states. "I just returned from the funeral services of five of the men not yet buried. It was odly [*sic*] conducted . . . deaths are quite frequent now. It is to be hoped that we will get out of this soon for a great many are sick." Their rations were also being cut as the war started to squeeze supplies for the Confederate armies. On May 20, 1862, he came one step closer to getting out of the stockade prisoner of war camp. A message was read from General Beauregard. It stated that all Shiloh prisoners were to be paroled, "except commishoned [*sic*] & non commishoned officers. . . ." Hadley was able to join the parole. On May 22, 1862, he left Camp Oglethorpe for the Union lines, first stopping off at a Nashville parole camp.

During his time at a parole camp in Nashville, Hadley thought more and more about going home. On July 4, 1862, safely behind Union lines, he saw no cause of celebration: "the fourth has certainly been a source of very little pleasure to me this morning. I went down the river with six or 7 boys, & had a good wash in the mingled waters of Mississippi & Ohio although it was quite muddy." Eight days later, on July 12, 1862, Hadley and the other Shiloh veterans from Camp Oglethorpe were sent to Benton Barracks in St. Louis, Missouri. Once again, he waited to continue the process of being paroled by the Union army, which would allow him to go home. Some men just did not wait for what they saw as a long process. Instead, they chose to escape from the camp. When orders were issued that any man who was not in camp would be charged with desertion, some of the same men trickled back into Benton Barracks.

Charles Whipple Hadley was mustered out of service on March 25, 1863, in St. Louis. The reason for his discharge was due to a disability. On his Disability Discharge papers, it describes an individual that had not been well for the last three months. Hadley was suffering from heart disease. It makes no mention that he was wounded during the battle of Shiloh. Hadley, when applying for a pension years later, stated that the root of his illnesses was in his words being, "kept in warehouses and old buildings, fed on condemned army rations, but mostly, cornmeal, at times a day without food, slept on the ground without cover or medical attention." He stated that the exception to this was his time spent at Camp Oglethorpe.

After being granted his discharge, Hadley left Benton Barracks and headed back to Anamosa to recuperate. Most likely, he returned to the home of his father, who was still practicing law. There is no indication that Hadley applied his trade as a teacher, which he listed in his military records when he joined the army. What is staggering is after his discharge for disabilities, he reenlisted in the Union army on October 12, 1864, serving again in the 14th Iowa Infantry Regiment, Company H. His enlistment lasted a little over a month when he was mustered out again on November 16, 1864, at Davenport, Iowa. Once again, he returned home and studied law with his father. Later in life, he used his experience with law to help him start a real estate career.

How Charles Whipple Hadley met his future wife is not recorded. She hailed from Ludlow, Windsor County, Vermont. Charles Hadley, by this time, was living in Owatonna, Minnesota, where his father now practiced law. He married Lille C. Adams on June 17, 1874. Their first child, a son, was christened Albert W. in 1877. The couple continued to live in Owatonna as late as 1880 on Cedar Street. In 1884, Charles applied for an invalid's pension citing "valvular disease of the heart." The pension office awarded the retirement at the rate of $16 a month, even though a pension investigator noted in the former soldier's paperwork that he found "no evidence of alleged disability."

Early in the next century, the family left Minnesota for Ogden, Utah, where Charles, with his son Albert, worked in the loan and real estate industry. According to the *Ogden Standard-Examiner*, on December 20, 1936, "he promoted the sale for the Southern Pacific railroad company all its Bear Valley river land." Hadley and his son did this by "running homestead excursions from the Midwest, conducting whole parties from the crowded Missouri, Kansas and Nebraska towns to the cheap, open, western country." His father also made a move to Ogden but passed away shortly after the family relocated.

Charles Whipple Hadley continued to prosper for the next three decades. He continued to work with his son in their loan and real estate business. On May 16, 1931, Lillie died, and two years later, their only surviving child, Albert W., died, leaving Charles distraught and alone. He had no family locally. In 1931, he asked for another increase in his pension, which the pension office granted, increasing his pension to $100. Although depressed, suffering both the war's physical and mental scars, Charles continued to work in his business. In 1935 Hadley requested another increase in his disability pension. A note was placed in his file from an investigator: "this pensioner owns his own home at the above address and has a housekeeper who looks after him. In addition to his home, he owns considerable property in Ogden, Utah, and takes care of his business affairs." The pension investigator continued, "he is said to be very close and shrewd financially."

The only person he had to look after him at home was a house-keeper, Mrs. Vanetta Martin. Every day she assisted at his home at 885

26th Street. It did not look as if he was going to receive another pension increase. On July 20, 1936, for reasons only known to Charles Whipple Hadley, he made his way to where he kept his trophy closet where he kept his prize gun collection. He took the firearm, raised it to his head, and pulled the trigger.

Mrs. Vanetta Martin ran to where she last saw Hadley. She then rushed toward the sound and found Hadley dead of a self-inflicted gunshot wound. Thus brought to a close the life of Charles Whipple Hadley of Anamosa, Iowa, the last of three Civil War veterans still living in Ogden, Utah. His body was taken by the local funeral parlor Larkin and Sons. After a brief funeral, his body was shipped back to Minnesota where he wished to be interred next to his wife and son in Owatonna, Steele County, Minnesota, in the Forest Hills Cemetery.

CHAPTER FOUR

The Howe Brothers (Orion and Lyston)

WILLIAM HARRISON HOWE WAS A FARMER FROM VERMONT WHO enlisted in the 2nd Infantry in Buffalo, New York. He signed on for five years on July 8, 1843. He lasted only three years as a private and musician. His discharge was on May 1, 1846. The reason stated for discharge was medical and related to a disability. His discharge did not describe the nature of his disability, but it resulted in him sitting out the Mexican-American War. After leaving the army, he moved out west to Portage County, Ohio.

While living in Portage, William Harrison Howe courted and sparked with Eliza Anna Westland. The two wed in 1847. Tragedy struck shortly after Eliza gave birth to her last child, born on August 27, 1850, in Hiram Rapids, Ohio. The couple named their son Lyston Durrett. Eliza died in 1852, leaving her husband William with two young sons to raise, including Orion Perseus, who had preceded his brother by about two years. Orion had been born on December 29, 1848, in Portage County, Ohio.

William Howe had little time to mourn. He continued to farm as most people did during that period. He also was a talented woodworker and supplemented his income as a cabinet maker. Being a widower did not last long; shortly after his wife Eliza died, he met a woman named Laura Maria Matteson. William and Laura wed in 1854. Contemporaries believed that the two did love each other; however, they also pointed out that William needed a mother to help raise his two young sons as much as he needed a companion.

Orion Howe

Youngest Soldier in Union Army
'61 to '65.

Born, Aug. 27, 1850.
Age; 10 years, 9 months and
9 days, at enlistment,

Co I - 15th Ills Vol Inf
Lyston D. Howe

Lyston Howe

Tragically, a year later, William found himself once again a widower. Laura died in 1855 shortly after giving birth to a son christened Wilfred Elon Howe. It was probably too much for William to bear. He decided to pack up his belongings, along with now three young sons. William waved goodbye to Ohio for Waukegan, Illinois, arriving there in 1857. It is believed the reason for the move was to be closer to a sister who could assist him with raising his three children. He eventually married for a third and final time in 1858 to Cordelia Sophia Partridge. William continued to earn a living farming and woodworking as he did in Ohio. His family eventually expanded by eight more children.

The Civil War commenced with the Confederate attack on Fort Sumter on April 13, 1861. Lincoln responded by calling for seventy-five thousand Union troops to be raised by volunteering.

> *Whereas the law of the United States have been for some time past, and now are opposed, and the execution thereof obstructed, in the States of South Carolina, Georgia, Alabama, Florida, Mississippi, Louisiana, and Texas, by combinations too powerful to be suppressed by the ordinary course of judicial proceedings, or by the powers vested in the marshals by law.*
>
> *Now, therefore, I, Abraham Lincoln, President of the United States, in virtue of the powers in me vested by the Constitution and the laws, have thought fit to call forth, and hereby do call forth, the militia of the several States of the Union to the aggregate number of seventy-five thousand, in order to suppress said combinations, and to cause the laws to be duly executed . . . .*

On April 16, 1861, Illinois governor Richard Yates called for "6,000 volunteers from his state."

The Howe family may have volunteered for service in the Civil War for a number of reasons. The Howes were likely ardently antislavery. They may have volunteered for the money as other Illinois natives did. Onley Andrus, who joined the 95th from McHenry County, about twenty-five miles away from Waukegan, wrote that he joined for the money. "I have been accused of being unsteady, and by those pretty near related to me too. Well as it is I am making money & in 3 years I shall have, if nothing happens, quite a little sum of money and with it, we can begin to live."

Fred Albert Shannon, a Civil War historian, believed that $13 a month pay was an incentive to someone who was down and out and did not own property. This might have also been an incentive for the two boys, or as many also cited, to preserve the Union. William and Lyston were the first in the family to take up the cause of the Union. Before enlisting in the army, Lyston, a musician, "drummed up recruits." He frequently traveled with his father to Chicago to inspire recruits.

Lyston joined the 15th Illinois Volunteer Infantry Company I on June 5, 1861, as a drummer. Soldiers below the age of eighteen were frequently taken on as drummers for a company. William Howe also enlisted in Company I. Roughly sixteen months later, on September 1, 1862, Orion, the oldest, joined the 55th Illinois Volunteer Infantry Company C, also as a drummer. In a short amount of time, all three ended up being united in the 55th Illinois but in different companies.

The 15th went, according to Lyston's biography in *Soldiers' and Patriots' Biographical Album*, to Freeport, Illinois, and joined the rest of the regiment at Benton Barracks or Camp Benton in St. Louis, Missouri, "where the regiment was organized under General John C. Freemont."

James K. Newton of the 14th Wisconsin wrote:

> *The real name is Benton Barracks but as we were in our tents and not in barracks we call it Camp Benton, so you see, the camp and the Barracks are separate from each other. The barracks were built last spring by General Freemont and calculated to hold 35,000 men.*

It was from there that they went to northwestern Missouri. Once in Missouri, the 15th was attached to Maj. Gen. Ulysses S. Grant's 21st Illinois, and with the 21st marched to Springfield, Missouri. During this time, Lyston was stricken with the black measles, a severe form of measles. He was sent to the hospital at Camp Hunter, Missouri, on October 19, 1861. When doctors observed him, they concluded there was nothing they could do for the little boy. Lyston was discharged from Camp Hunter to die at home. Despite the grim prognosis, he made a miraculous recovery. In February 1862, he reenlisted, this time in the 55th Illinois Infantry Company B. His stepmother did her best to dissuade Lyston from leaving. She felt that marching and the hardship of army life, coupled with his youth, took too much of a toll on the boy. When he left, she resigned herself to the fact she would never see him alive again. Meanwhile, as Lyston recovered, his brother Orion was just starting out in his army career.

In his pension request located in the National Archives, Orion testified that he was thirteen when he enlisted and not sixteen. He insisted that he lied so he would be able to join the army. Orion Howe, a musician, described himself in 1862 "as 4'11", light complexion with brown hair and hazel eyes." Surviving records indicate that Orion was similar in height and appearance to his father. Orion successfully enlisted in the 55th Illinois on September 1, 1862. He was mustered into Company C. Once again, William also served in the 55th, but again in a different company. His father transferred due to a promotion to a fife major. William's job was to organize, select, and train the drummers in the regiment.

On February 6, 1862, Grant had attacked Fort Henry in Tennessee, on the Tennessee River. A week later, Grant attacked Fort Donelson, located on the Cumberland River. Once these forts were secured, they would open up Tennessee to Union forces and keep Kentucky loyal to the Union. Grant's successes allowed the Union to strike at Rebel supply routes as well as Rebel railroads. Once the Union conquered these forts, General Grant continued to Pittsburg Landing, on the Tennessee River. William and Lyston would be in the battle of their lives near a small church named Shiloh.

According to the 55th Ilinois Regimental History, on March 16, 1862, with the rest of the brigade to which it belonged, the regiment filed up the hill from Pittsburg Landing to the woods west of the landing. The following morning, each soldier was ordered to take three days' rations and forty rounds of ammunition. They continued the march "along the Hamburg Road near Locust Creek." It was here that the 55th Illinois camped near a peach orchard. The 54th Ohio Infantry camped close to the 55th Illinois, and beyond the 54th was the 71st Ohio Infantry at the junction of the Hamburg and Purdy Roads.

While General Grant's troops were in camp near Pittsburg Landing, they were attacked by Confederate forces under the command of Gen. Albert Sidney Johnston. The Confederate general wanted to attack the Union forces before Maj. Gen. Don Carlos Buell could reinforce Grant. If Buell joined Grant, it would swell Union troops to over sixty thousand. Johnston chose to attack in the early morning hours of April 6, 1862, near Shiloh Church with about forty-five thousand soldiers.

Private Elisha Stockwell Jr., another child soldier but with the 14th Wisconsin Infantry, recorded that the battle commenced "on Sunday morning, April 6, 1862, I was on camp guard, and a little after sunrise heard musket firing up the river toward Pittsburg Landing. . . ." Confederates poured out of the woods and attacked the Union soldiers, compelling them to fall back toward the river. Jonathan Catlin of the 52nd Illinois wrote in his diary:

> *The Rebels made a general attack on early Sunday morning, we fought them hard all day, when came on we lost a great deal of ground and cut up badly, we lay Sunday night on the banks of the river, it rained very hard in the night, but we were up and at them in the morning early and after some hard fighting succeeded in driving them from our grounds we meeting them with but very little loss.*

According to Lyston's memory, recorded in *Soldiers and Patriots* and published in 1892, the "55th was flanked by the 54th Ohio on the right." The 71st Ohio, which was at the front lines, broke, and they began to retreat. The 55th continued to fight with Lyston, who swapped his instrument for a musket and found himself in what was termed the "Hornet's Nest." The National Park Service, which oversees the battlefield, describes Shiloh's Hornet's Nest as a "nearly six-hundred-yard stretch of what came to be known as the Sunken Road in the center of the battlefield and was the scene of heavy combat on both days of the battle."

Eventually establishing a line, the Union artillery held the Confederate attack while Buell's recruits began to arrive. A tremendous loss occurred for the Confederates when a bullet clipped General Johnston's femoral artery, causing death quickly. Gen. P. G. T. Beauregard replaced the mortally wounded Johnston. When the Army of Ohio arrived, it helped Grant drive the Confederates from the field. A soldier from the 11th Indiana Infantry wrote on April 7, 10:00 a.m.:

Our whole army made a general advance and continued to advance slowly keeping up a heavy fire, till 12:00 pm. When the rebels made a last desperate stand when the most desperate fighting took place that ever was done on this continent. The musketry actually drowned the artillery fire, the very earth seemed to tremble.

Beauregard realized the cause lost and ordered his troops to retreat.

Newton later wrote to his family, "there is no use in trying to describe the battle because I can not do it." One can only imagine what Lyston saw, as another soldier wrote of the battle:

The first dead man we saw was a short distance from the clearing. He was leaning back against a big tree as if asleep, but his intestines were all over his legs and several times their natural size. I didn't look at him the second time as it made me deathly sick.

According to Lyston's biography, the 55th Regiment then moved toward Corinth. It assisted in its siege, and after its evacuation, moved to Memphis, passing through Grand Junction to Holly Springs, arriving there July 21, 1862.

Shiloh was part of a broader military strategy implemented shortly after the start of the Civil War. It became apparent to those in the military command that the war would be a prolonged conflict. Lt. Gen. Winfield Scott, commander of the army for many years, wrote to both Gen. George McClellan and President Abraham Lincoln about what he believed would eventually bring the Confederacy to its knees. His plan, he wrote on April 27, 1861, would help to take the pressure off Washington, DC, from a Confederate attack. The press mocked General Scott's plan, which was dubbed the Anaconda Plan because it resembled a constrictor snake that slowly strangles and crushes its prey.

General Scott proposed a complete blockade of all the ports on the Confederacy's East Coast and the Gulf Coast to prevent needed supplies from moving freely between Europe and the Confederate States of America. The plan initially did not have the support of many of the Union commanders. They hoped to invade and defeat the South, not strangle it.

The Mississippi River played the same role in Scott's plan that the Hudson River played during the American Revolution. It was believed that in the western half of the Confederacy, absolute control of the Mississippi River and its tributaries was crucial. If the Federal forces could control the Mississippi, it would effectively split the eastern Confederacy from the western half of the Confederacy. Western Louisiana, Texas, and Arkansas would be isolated. Communication would be halted, and supply chains and movement of troops would be affected. It would be a psychological defeat for the Confederacy. If secured, the Mississippi would allow Union territories in the West to ship needed troops to the East.

Even though Scott retired from the army in November 1861, his plan continued to be implemented in 1862 and 1863 with the Vicksburg Campaign. Without controlling the strategically important city of Vicksburg, the Union could not entirely control the Mississippi. It was known to be heavily defended. Jefferson Davis, the president of the Confederate States of America, referred to Vicksburg as "the nailhead that held the South's two halves together." Lincoln, equally impressed by its importance, stated that in his opinion, "See what a lot of land these fellows hold, of which Vicksburg is the key. The war can never be brought to a close until that key is in our pocket." He continued that Vicksburg was more important than New Orleans.

The momentum continued for the Union army and navy. On April 5, 1862, New Orleans, Louisiana, fell, followed by Memphis, Tennessee, on June 6. The Union controlled both ends of the Mississippi River in the West. This allowed General Grant to push toward Vicksburg's objective, which meant total control of the Mississippi and splitting the Confederacy.

While Lyston had been at the earlier siege of Corinth on October 3 and 4, 1862, the following year Orion was part of two significant assaults. The first launched on May 19, 1863, and the second three days later, on the 22nd. Orion and the 55th Illinois were sent down the Graveyard Road, one of Vicksburg's main roads. Standing in their way was the Stockade Redan, a triangular fortification with a "V" facing the direction of the attacking force. The night before the attack on the redan, the regiments "lay under arms in a cornfield within musket range of the fortifications." The assault began before daybreak. The men encountered "stumps, limbs and fallen trees," on their way.

According to the *Vicksburg Post*, "At 2 p.m., May 19, 1863, soldiers in a corps commanded by Union [Major] Gen. William T. Sherman attacked Stockade Redan along Graveyard Road." In his memoirs, Sherman stated, "the parapets were strongly manned and the enemy fought hard and well." His losses were pretty heavy. According to Mike Sigalas, who wrote *Vicksburg: A Guided Tour through History*, "Sherman tried to overwhelm the Stockade Redan itself, sending men straight up the parapet walls all along the redan." The 55th Illinois, and the 54th Ohio were part of the charge. Descending on the redan toward Vicksburg was a fourteen-year-old drummer, sometimes fifer Orion Perseus Howe of the 55th Illinois Infantry Company C. The company found themselves pinned down by fire from the redan. "A few soldiers made it to the wall of the redan but had no ladders with which to scale it. They remained stranded there for hours, waiting on the night to set in so they could retreat."

Orion Howe was described by his comrades as follows: "He drummed well, proved hardy, never seemed homesick." He passed through battle after battle, and march after march "untouched by disease, unscathed by bullet and shell." During the battle of May 19, 1863, Howe wore a white handkerchief tied about the left arm. This told troops he was a noncombatant. He mainly stayed in the rear to assist with the wounded.

When bullets became exhausted, Orion was told to start collecting cartridges from the dead and wounded. Once enough were gathered, he brought them to the front, where they were distributed among the soldiers. Eventually, all the ammunition was exhausted, and Orion was ordered to head to the rear where extra ammunition was being kept. The regimental history of the 55th recounted the boy's ordeal.

*We could see him nearly all the way . . . he ran through what seemed
a hailstorm of canister and musket balls, each throwing up its little
puff of dust when it struck dry hillside. Suddenly he dropped and
hearts sank, but he had only tripped. After he stumbled sometimes,
he fell prostrate but was quickly up again and he finally disappeared
from us, limping over the summit and the 55th saw him no more for
several months.*

Finally, a bullet found his right leg, and Orion Howe fell. This time
it took him what seemed like forever to get back on his feet. The pain
was excruciating, but he could not let the men counting on him to bring
back ammunition down. Slowly he got back to his feet; he noticed he was
bleeding heavily. As he continued his journey, Minié balls whizzed by
him, making various noises, like buzzing insects, as they flew past his ears.
Finally, he arrived before General Sherman. Dizzy from loss of blood,
thirsty, and out of breath, Orion still managed to address the general,
"General Sherman send some cartridges to Colonel [Oscar] Malmborg,
the men are all out." After hearing what the young boy had to say, Sherman looked down at Orion's leg with his pant leg stained red; he saw that
Howe was wounded. The general called for a litter to take the musician to
the rear for medical treatment without acknowledging the request.

Watching this situation unfold was the son of General Grant,
twelve-year-old Frederick "Fred" Grant. He wrote in 1898:

*A small boy, with blood streaming from a wound in his leg, came
running up to where my father and Sherman stood, and reported
that his regiment was out of ammunition. Sherman was directing
some attention to be paid to his wound, when the little fellow, finding
himself fainting from loss of blood, gasped out, "Calibre 56," as he was
carried off to the rear. At this moment I observed that my father's eyes
were filled out tears.*

Orion refused to be removed from in front of the general. He insisted
not only that the general acknowledge his request, but he wanted to
walk himself to the rear not be carried. Just before he took his leave of

the general, Howe yelled out that the calibre of ammunition needed was "Calibre .54." It was a smaller caliber than required for the guns, but rifles begin to foulwith dirt and grime from the black powder. A smaller caliber would allow the muskets to work under the conditions. Ultimately the Illinois 55th was forced to retreat, forcing Grant to rethink the taking of Vicksburg. According to some historians, including Eleanor C. Bishop, the caliber requested was recorded wrong in the story. The correct caliber was .58. However, the .54 version of the story was more romantic.

After being wounded, "by gunshot in the fleshy part of the right thigh," Orion Howe went to a hospital where he eventually recovered. He returned home on leave for thirty days starting on June 5, 1863, until he was finally discharged on February 17, 1864, in Chicago, Illinois. Howe reenlisted in the 55th Illinois Infantry again as a veteran on February 14, 1864, with Capt. Francis Shaw. He was fifteen years old and assigned as an orderly for Maj. Gen. Giles A. Smith. Orderlies helped the general in his day to day duties. Howe moved dispatches between skirmish lines during the Battle of Dallas, which was fought between May 26 and June 4, 1864.

This battle was part of Sherman's Atlanta Campaign. Lt. Gen. William J. Hardee of the Confederate States of America and Maj. Gen. John A. Logan of the Union army led the opposing forces. Howe, in the execution of his duties, was shot twice, once in the right arm and then once in the chest. He was moved off the field of battle to a field hospital. When it was felt that he stabilized, Orion was furloughed home. Pvt. Orion P. Howe was honorably discharged in New York City on October 5, 1864, by Special Order 327 from the War Department Adjutant General Office.

His brother Lyston like Orion became an orderly, but for Maj. Gen. William Babcock Hazen. He was assigned this duty in July 1864, and remained with Major General Hazen until he too was discharged from the army the following year on March 27, 1865, in Goldsboro, North Carolina. His last campaign was also the Atlanta Campaign with General Sherman. After being mustered out of the military, "newspapers reported he was crippled with rheumatism and unable to walk." Lyston returned home by steamer to Baltimore and then by rail to Chicago. A local newspaper reported that Lyston "was brought home on a stretcher at the close of the war." It took him two years before he was able to walk on his own again. Once able to ambulate, he helped his father on their farm, who mustered out earlier than both boys.

Orion P. Howe was eventually recommended as a suitable candidate to attend West Point in New York's Hudson River Valley. However, he was too young to attend. Instead, on July 28, 1865, he accepted an appointment to the Naval Academy in Annapolis, Maryland. The recommendation was made by Gen. William Tecumseh Sherman, who remembered Orion's brave actions on May 19, 1863.

His acceptance into the academy was deferred to allow him to study for the entrance exams. Orion P. Howe eventually entered the academy as a midshipman. He resigned from the academy on June 15, 1867. When looking through his records from his time at the Naval Academy, it is apparent it was due to grades in arithmetic and algebra, which are listed as deficient. He was sixteen years old when he left the academy. In his memoirs, Sherman recorded that "he could not graduate, and I do not know what has become of him." After leaving, some sources state that he joined the Merchant Marine and was assigned to the ship *Thornton*, which was wrecked off Ireland's coast in November 1867.

Once back in the United States, Orion and Lyston were harness and saddle makers for a short time. According to the 1870 US Federal Census, Orion pursued those trades in Parkville, Missouri. Orion seemed to have abandoned that endeavor as he traveled to Texas, where he became a cowboy. Lyston pursued another path, starting work for the railroad first as a brakeman on the C & A Railroad, becoming a switchman, and finally a yardmaster in Braidwood, Illinois.

Lyston made his way to Streator, Illinois, where he became a receiver for the Pekin & South Western Railroad, which ran from Pekin to Joliet, Illinois. He married Marion Wiley Stewart in 1873. The couple had three sons: Orion, Lyston, and Arthur. Lyston, according to the *Streator Times*, is credited with originating a coal washing process. He "built facilities along the C.B.&Q Railroad on Otter Creek." He had a coal washer there as well as coke ovens. There was not enough water for his needs, and he was forced to move his operation to the Vermillion River and Wilmington on the Kankakee River. His last relocation was to Central City, where farmers complained that the coal washing process's dust was killing their crops. Growing tired of the conflict, he sold the business to a railroad and purchased the Hamilton & Russell Hardware store in Streator, and finally retired in 1918.

Orion married Ellen Mitchell on June 17, 1879. The couple had two children, Lyston D., born in Missouri in 1880, and Ella, born two years later in Illinois. Shortly after Ella's birth, his wife died. He married Mary (Maria) Eva Stephan on June 3, 1886, and they remained married until she died in 1916, although toward the end of her life, they were listed as separated. He concisely summed up the reason for their separation: "we have agreed to disagree, she has money, and I have not." In the 1880 census, he was listed again as a harness maker.

In 1890 Orion relocated to New York City, where he applied and was accepted to the New York City School of Dentistry, which would eventually merge with New York University in 1925. Orion attended the school from 1890 to 1892, where he graduated in 1892.

After dental school, Orion moved to 186 Linwood Avenue in Buffalo, New York, where he lived with his children. He relocated to Sutton, Nebraska, by 1896. This same year President Cleveland "allowed for Civil War units to nominate additional soldiers for the Medal of Honor." Orion P. Howe's name was submitted, and as a direct consequence, he was awarded the Medal of Honor for the May 1863 attack on the Stockade Redan. He was given his medal on April 23, 1896. One of Howe's fellow members of the 55th wrote, "I have a distinct recollection of the wound rec'd by him in the leg during the assault on Vicksburg about May 19th or 20th 1863 while carrying a message from the colonel to Genl Sherman. The injury was a severe flesh wound although I have forgotten the particulars."

By 1904, Orion P. Howe was living in Clay Center, Kansas. He was still making a living as a dentist. However, by 1912, Orion returned to Buffalo, New York, residing at 258 Lexington Avenue, according to the directory listing the residents, where they lived, their occupations, and sometimes their places of business. One of the reasons he had left Buffalo was because of the chest wound received in the Battle of Dallas. The bullet pierced one of his lungs, and since then, he had been susceptible to illness. He blamed this on the northern climate, which sometimes did not agree with him. As he aged, his old wounds disabled him more until, in 1912, he applied for an increase in his pension.

He explained that he was "totally blind and very much in need of his increase." During this time, he was also suffering from heart disease. He dictated the letter to the Pension Bureau to his attorney, who wrote it for him. His blindness also prevented him from continuing to work as a dentist. His requested increase was also related to the act of May 11, 1912, allowing for the possibility of a hike in veterans' pensions. The following year he was awarded a total of $30 a month. In the New York State Census for 1915, Orion still resided in Buffalo on Cleaveland Street with his wife. His wife passed away the following year on February 2, 1916.

Orion P. Howe's health continued to decline. During the last years of his life, he was periodically confined to hospitals such as St. Joseph's Hospital. In addition to being almost entirely blind, he suffered from an ailment described as a palsy or tremor. Increasingly feeble, Orion decided to move back to Missouri to be near his daughter. She did her best to make him comfortable. The last census listing Orion P. Howe was in 1920. It recorded him as living in Colorado. His pension continued to increase after more claims were requested.

Corp. Orion P. Howe died on January 27, 1930. In a letter to the federal government, his daughter asked for $312 for his burial and an accompanying military stone. He was interred in the Springfield National Cemetery. The year his brother died Lyston was still a hardware merchant in Streator, Illinois, where he lived with Marion. Two years after Orion's death, Marion died. Lyston lived until January 13, 1937, when he suffered a fall; he was taken to St. Mary's Hospital, where he died. Lyston was interred at the Riverview Cemetery in Streator, Illinois. His surviving children made an application for a military headstone like that of his brother. It is believed that he was the youngest soldier to serve in Illinois during the Civil War.

CHAPTER FIVE

William H. Horsfall (Medal of Honor)

WILLIAM H. HORSFALL WAS BORN ON MARCH 3, 1847, IN NEWPORT, Kentucky, the son of Jonathan Thomas Horsfall and his wife, Elizabeth Ann McDowell. When the Civil War started, William, only fourteen years old, decided that he wanted adventure. What better way than to join the Union army to preserve the nation. According to *Deeds of Valor* by Walter F. Beyer, Horsfall remembered, "I left home without money or warning to my parents, and in company with three other boys, stealthily boarded the steamer *Annie Laurie* moored at the Cincinnati wharf at Newport and billed for the Kanawha River that evening about the 20th of December 1861." When the boat was ready to set off, his friends fled back to the safety of the shore after having a change of heart. Many years later, William remembered the other boys tried to convince him to join them back onshore. He promptly refused.

When the *Annie Laurie* pushed off from its mooring, William H. Horsfall remained hidden. Perhaps growing hungry, he ventured out of his hiding place to explore the ship. The ship captain, patrolling his boat, caught the young stowaway. Once he realized that Horsfall was a stowaway, the captain became irate with Horsfall. William pleaded to the captain's better side, explaining that he was an orphan and the reason for his stowing away on the *Annie Laurie*. The ship captain had a change of heart and took good care of Horsfall.

According to William's account, he enlisted in the Union army on January 1, 1862. He became a drummer in the First Regiment Kentucky Volunteers Company G, at Camp Cox, Virginia, which is now part of

Charleston, West Virginia. William was small for his age, 4' 3" with blue eyes and light hair. It was because of his age and height that he became a drummer boy for the 1st Kentucky. He was given the rank of private. His first major battle would occur about three months later at Pittsburg Landing in Tennessee, better known as the Battle of Shiloh.

After the Battle of Shiloh, on April 6 and 7, 1862, the defeated Confederate army under the command of Gen. P. G. T. Beauregard, along with sixty-five thousand soldiers, retreated from Shiloh to the railroad hub of Corinth, in northeast Mississippi. Shiloh had been an effort to defend Corinth and the "Memphis and Charleston rail which ran east and west and the Mobile and Ohio railroad running North and South." These rail lines were vital to the Confederates in bringing supplies and troops to different areas during the war and were also an essential component in defending the Mississippi Valley.

A Union army under the command of Maj. Gen. Henry W. Halleck with one hundred twenty thousand soldiers started south, intending to take the town of Corinth. On April 30, 1862, the Union army moved slowly toward Corinth. Private Horsfall would put down his drum and pick up a rifle during a skirmish on May 21, 1862, at Widow Serratt's located near Corinth. Col. Thomas D. Sedgewick of the 2nd Kentucky Infantry filed a report almost a month later on June 20, 1862, in the camp outside Corinth. Sedgewick wrote from the headquarters of the 22nd Brigade camp near Corinth, Mississippi, on June 20, 1862, that he was ordered to "make a forced reconnaissance with my brigade in front of General Wood's division. Colonel Sedgewick moved forward with four regiments to Driver's house. He was 'joined by a battery of artillery and a squandron of cavalry from General Wood's divison.' The four regiments moved ahead of Generals Wood's and Sherman's divisions." The First Kentucky Regiment was on the left of the road, which led to Corinth. The 20th Kentucky was on the right of the road. Sedgwick detached two companies from each regiment to act as skirmishers.

In front of the 20th Kentucky was an open field. The Confederate army occupied a dense wood near the field. The 1st Kentucky was placed in thick woods. As soon as the skirmishers started forward, they were fired on by the Confederates in the woods. The Kentucky soldiers eventually were able to gain ground and take up a position in front of Widow Serratt's house. It was not held long because the Confederate soldiers rallied to push the Union soldiers back. This happened at least three times, according to Sedgwick's report. He then called forward "two additional companies from their regiments to their support, with orders to press forward." He also ordered up heavy artillery as well as cavalry in the rear. The battery was placed on a "high ridge commanding the woods in front occupied by the enemy." Finally, the 2nd Kentucky Infantry was moved forward with the 31st Indiana Regiment.

Colonel Sedgwick believed that the Confederates intended to turn "our left flank, which was held by three companies of the First Kentucky, under the command of Captain Wheeler." Eventually, with the arrival of other companies and unleashing a fury of artillery on the woods, the enemy fell back only to rally three more times. Captain Wheeler with the 1st Kentucky was able to hold his ground. During one of these rallies, "Captain Williamson and 17 men of the First Kentucky fell wounded, some mortally." Capt. James T. Williamson was severely wounded with a bullet wound to his hip. Even in pain and badly injured, he continued to direct the movements of his men.

Pvt. William H. Horsfall was a sniper during this battle. Many years later, he remembered that "my position was to the right of the First Kentucky, as an independent sharpshooter." He was approached by Lieutenant Hocke, who told Private Horsfall, "Captain Williamson is in a serious predicament; rescue him if possible." Horsfall was successful in making his way to the wounded officer. He was able to drag the injured Williamson to a stretcher. Once on the stretcher, he was taken to the rear for treatment. According to another report by Maj. Frank P. Cahill of the 1st Kentucky, the engagement lasted about two hours. No mention was made of the heroic actions that day of Pvt. William H. Horsfall. However, Maj. Gen. William S. Rosecrans saw the heroic action and commended him for it.

After the Siege of Corinth, the 1st Kentucky was part of the occupation forces that held the town. On July 1, 1862, the 1st Kentucky participated in the Battle of Boonville, which occurred when Confederate general Braxton Bragg tried to recapture Corinth, Mississippi.

In November and December of 1862, Willaim H. Horsfall was listed on the muster rolls as sick. He was not present in camp but sent to a hospital in Nashville, Tennessee. What he was ill with is unknown, but the water in and around Corinth was not clean. Many men would succumb to illness. He would be back in time for the battle of Stone's River or the Second Battle of Murfreesboro, on December 31, 1862.

During a charge, Private Horsfall became surrounded by Rebel infantry and cavalry. It looked as if he would be taken prisoner. One Confederate decided he was going to shoot Horsfall down. Someone noticed how young the boy was, and the soldier was told not to fire on Horsfall. While the Confederates were deciding what to do with Horsfall, William made a successful escape back to the Union lines' safety. The next time he would not be so lucky.

William was captured on September 10, 1863, in Graysville, Georgia. In the National Archives, his service records list him as "not stated" from July 1863 to February 1864. He is listed as present again in March-April 1864, with the notation that he will be discharged. On June 18, 1864, it was written in his service record "time not expired not mustered out, turned over to Provost Marshall at Covington, Ky." He was finally discharged on August 19, 1864 at Louisville, Kentucky. A notation stated "per S.O.# 249 par.39. War Department, A.G.O. dated July 26, 1864 by way of favor." He reenlisted in the Union army on March 1, 1865, in Company K 4th Regiment of the US Volunteers in Cincinnati, Ohio, for a $400 sign-on bonus. William remained in the US Army until he was discharged on March 1, 1866. After discharge, he returned to Newport, Kentucky.

On September 6, 1871, William H. Horsfall married Laura B. Tucker in Cincinnati, Ohio. They would have six children. His wife would die on August 14, 1897. He married again, and his last wife listed on his death certificate was named Lucretia. Gary A. Casson wrote in the *Encyclopedia of Northern Kentucky* that Horsfall "suffered most of his life from rheumatism and pain in his lungs, back, and limbs as well as from heart disease." The same article cites that after the war he was a notary public and wrote poems about the war, composed music, and sang songs about the war.

He was a semi-invalid after the war, and he applied for a pension with the US government. In 1889 he put in a pension application, which would be increased over the years. Before 1890, he was given $30 a month, and by 1920, it would be doubled. As early as 1893, he cited that he needed a personal aide to help him in life's daily activities. He was unable to perform light manual labor. William continued that " he is constantly confined to his bed and house." His final request was that he not be examined by a local doctor because they "won't help his cause." He was just forty-six years old. His home, according to the census and pension applications, was at 167 Liberty Street in Newport, Kentucky. He still remained active in veterans groups, including becoming commander of the William Nelson Post of the Grand Army of the Republic. In 1893, his heroism in pulling Captain Williamson to safety was finally recognized when he was awarded the Medal of Honor. He was presented with the medal on August 17, 1895.

William H. Horsfall died October 22, 1922, at his home at 218 West Third Street in Newport, Kentucky. The funeral was held at his home, and afterward, his burial was at the Evergreen Cemetery in the Grand Army of the Republic's plots. His wife, Lucretia Horsfall, died one year later in 1923.

Today there is a historical marker testifying to the exploits and life of William H. Horsfall, one of the youngest recipients of the Medal of Honor during the Civil War.

Chapter Six

Alexander H. Johnson
(Drummer for the 54th)

Boston, Massachusetts, unveiled a monument to the 54th Massachusetts Infantry over three decades after the battle at Fort Wagner on May 3, 1897. The dedication day was Memorial Day. The sculptor, Augustus Saint-Gaudens, created the sculpture commemorating the 54th Massachusetts. It would be placed where the 54th commenced its march on the Boston Common. It was made of bronze, and at the front of the regiment it depicted Col. Robert Gould Shaw and beside him a sixteen-year-old drummer named Alexander Howard Johnson. Although Johnson was once widely considered the first African-American musician to enlist in the Union army, it is now believed that this probably is not true. He, however, was perhaps one of the earliest.

Alexander Johnson was born on April 23, 1846. Although some had listed him as sixteen years old when he enlisted in the 54th Regiment, many believe he was fourteen. His obituary in the *Springfield Republican* is one such source that lists him as fourteen years old at the time of his enlistment. Sometime around 1850, it is believed he became separated from his parents. He was declared an orphan. His father was "the son of a Narragansett Indian, and his mother was Irish-Indian whose father was a Montauk Indian." He was separated from his parents, and why is not entirely apparent to those who have researched his life.

William Henry Johnson, a prominent African-American lawyer, and his wife, Hannah, adopted Alexander. William H. Johnson was well

Alexander H. Johnson

known as the second African-American lawyer in the United States. Alexander's father also was well known in New Bedford, Massachusetts, as an abolitionist, counting among his close friends the great orator Frederick Douglass. Johnson spent the first part of his life in New Bedford. He most likely attended school because in later US censuses the enumerator recorded that he could read and write. According to the last federal census before the Civil War, Alexander lived in the 3rd Ward, in New Bedford, in the County of Bristol.

There is little known about his years before the Civil War and enlistment in the 54th Massachusetts Regiment. A drummer was the logical choice for him. In later interviews, Alexander H. Johnson remembered he loved to play the drum as far back as he could remember. According to Meserette Kentake in her article "Alexander H. Johnson: The First Drummer Boy," Johnson stated in an interview that he "'beat a drum everyday he has been able since childhood.'" He was quite good at it. The following year the Civil War would commence. Alexander's desire to join the Union army was influenced not only by his father but by the family's association with Frederick Douglass and his sons. One of Douglass's sons would briefly be in the 54th Massachusetts Infantry along with Alexander. Researchers of Alexander's life also believe that John Brown's Raid influenced his decision to join the Union army.

Alexander officially joined the 54th as a musician on March 2, 1863. He would be mustered formally on March 30, 1863. Private Johnson received a $50 enlistment bonus and would be assigned to Company C. He listed his occupation on his enlistment papers as a seaman. He had tried to join the Union army earlier, it is believed, in 1861, but because of his age, he probably was not officially part of a regiment until 1863, the same year the 54th was formed. Almost three months after enlisting, the 54th left Boston for James Island, South Carolina. When he joined the 54th, Johnson was quite a gifted musician.

According to the Massachusetts Historical Society, The Regiment left camp on the 28 of May 1863 for Boston. They left Boston on the transport De Molay. In an article about him, David "Chet" Williamson Sneade wrote that "Before leaving Boston to march among the ranks of the 54th, Col. Edward M. Hollowell presented Johnson with a brass drum." According to the regimental history of the 54th, Frederick Douglass stood on the pier to bid the soldiers farewell. Some noticed that Douglass remained on the dock until the transport with the 54th on it was well out of sight. The transport reached Hilton Head, South Carolina, on June 2, 1863. It is recorded in the 54th regimental history that they then went into camp at Thompsons Plantations near Beaufort, South Carolina, on June 4, and July 8, "the regiment proceeded to Stono Inlet where they would be involved in their first battle."

When the 54th arrived in South Carolina, their first engagement would occur on July 16, 1863. Kentake, in the same interview with Alexander H. Johnson, reported his words: "'We fought from 7 in the morning to 4:40 in the afternoon, and we succeeded in driving the enemy back. After the battle, we got a paper saying that if Fort Wagner was charged within a week it would be taken.'" They would attack Fort Wagner on Morris Island on July 18, 1863. "'Most of the way we were singing, Col. Shaw and I marching at the head of the regiment. It was getting dark when we crossed the bridge to Morris Island. It was about 6:30 o'clock when we got there.'" The order to storm Fort Wagner was given an hour later.

The Battery Wagner helped defend Charlestown Harbor. Using heavy artillery, they created a gauntlet for enemy ships attempting to enter the harbor. Col. Robert Gould Shaw led the charge with the 54th, capturing the outer rifle pits surrounding the fort. The 54th was able, with other regiments, to enter the actual fort only to be pushed back. Instead of a frontal assault, the Union created a siege. After about two months of almost constant bombardment, Fort Wagner fell on September 7, 1863. During the initial charge, Colonel Shaw was killed, as were almost three hundred men of the 54th. This attack was immortalized in the movie *Glory*.

Pvt. Alexander H. Johnson would spend the remainder of the Civil War in the 54th Regiment. He would see plenty of action during his time with the 54th, including being wounded in the leg and having his drum destroyed several times. In addition to being in the siege of Charleston from August 17 to September 7, 1863, he would be involved in the Battle of Olustee in February 1864, and Honey Hill in November 1864. He recollected in an interview in a local newspaper that, "'We were told there was a price on the head of every colored man before we fought the battle of Honey Hill. The Union man were forced to retreat and our regiment was left to the enemy, while others were retreating. . . .'" It would be a Confederate victory. This battle occurred during Sherman's March to the Sea. Johnson participated in the fight of Boykin's Mills in April 1865 and again in the Battle of James Island in 1865. On August 20, 1865, a 5' 2" sixteen-year-old, Johnson, as stated on his discharge papers, left the Union army in Charleston, South Carolina. He headed back to his home in New Bedford, Massachusetts.

After the war, Johnson left New Bedford and moved to Worcester, Massachusetts. According to David "Chet" William Sneade, in his blog post, "Jazz Riffing on a Lost Worcester: The Rhythm of the 54th," Johnson spent the next sixty years in Worcester. He continued to drum and brought his wartime drum with him to Worcester. Here he started a drum corp where he was the drum major. He frequently wore his forage cap from the late war and people called him "The Major."

Early in his residence in Worcester, he met his future wife, Mary A. Johnson (no relation). He married her on February 24, 1870. The couple would have seventeen children. The 1870 US Census lists Alexander's occupation as a waiter and his age as twenty-three. When not working, he was drumming. In an interview quoted by Sneade, Johnson stated about the drum corp he founded, "'It surely was heard from. It had 22 pieces, all snare drums, except one that was a bass drum.'" When they practiced, the buildings around their practice room shook with the sounds and vibration. These drum corps were a regular feature in parades in which Alexander and his band were happy to play. In a 1920 interview in a local Worcester newspaper, he proudly told the reporter that he was teaching his grandson to play the drum.

Alexander remained active in George H. Ward Post #10, Grand Army of the Republic. He also belonged to the Sons of Union Veterans of the Civil War in Worcester. Johnson was aware of the monument to the 54th that had been unveiled on Memorial Day in 1897. He would not get a chance to view it until the early part of the twentieth century. His obituary stated: "His familiar figure appears in bas relief in bronze in Civil War uniform holding his drum and drum sticks marching in martial army, together with his comrades. . . ." How many times he visited the site is not known.

Johnson and his wife lived out their days in Worcester. Many of the couple's seventeen children died early in life. One child named Alexander Howard Johnson Jr. died in 1875 from fever and pneumonia, at a little over a year. Perhaps the love he derived from drumming and music, in general, helped ease the pain of the loss of his children.

By 1880 Johnson resided at 69 Central Street and listed his occupation as a carpet cleaner. On March 11, 1889, he applied for a pension for his time served with the 54th Massachusetts Infantry Regiment. His last residence was 21 Orchard Street, which is where he lived by 1910. During this time, he listed his occupation as a laborer in a factory and a wage earner. The enumerator noted that he had been out of work for eighteen weeks. Ten years later, he was still living at the same address.

"Major" Alexander H. Johnson died on March 19, 1930, from "paralytic shock suffered last November." The drummer boy of the 54th Massachusetts Regiment was buried in the Grand Army of the Republic's plot in Hope Cemetery in Worcester, Massachusetts. His simple military headstone read, "Musn A.H. Johnson Co. C 54 Mass. Inf." According to his obituary, the funeral featured a large gathering who mourned the loss and was complete with a police escort, a large contingent of the Grand Army of the Republic, and, of course, a drum corp.

CHAPTER SEVEN

Lola Sanchez (Confederate Spy)

THE AMERICAN CIVIL WAR AFFECTED ALL SEGMENTS OF THE US POP-
ulation, including Hispanics, who would be represented on both sides of
the conflict. The National Park Service estimates that "by the close of the
war, more than 20,000 Hispanics had participated in the bloody conflict"
known as the American Civil War. Maria "Lola" Dolores Sanchez was a
notable Confederate spy.

Sanchez was born on September 15, 1844, in Armstrong, Florida.
She was the daughter of Cuban immigrants who came to Florida when
she was about five years old. She would have probably remained out of
the Civil War, but her father, Don Mauricio Sanchez, was arrested for
being a Confederate by Union soldiers in the vicinity of their home. He
maintained his innocence but was still confined in prison. It was because
he was "a spy" that their family home was confiscated. Complicating matters is that he had a son already in the Confederate army. Don Sanchez
was jailed at Fort San Marco in St. Augustine. Lola continued to live in
their home with her three sisters, another brother, and her mother, Maria,
an invalid.

The family was well off. According to the 1850 US Census, her father
was listed as a farmer with a real estate value of $2,000. On the eve of the
Civil War in 1860, the census recorded that he had a real estate value of
$3,500 and a personal value of $5,200. The family, according to Valerie
D. Aguilar in her online history, lived in a decent-sized home on the
"East bank of the St. John's River." This was opposite Palatka, Florida,
which was a busy shipping area. While the Union officers boarded at the

Sanchez home, the family waited on them and cooked for the officers and sometimes their wives. It was a humiliating experience for sure.

While waiting on the officers during dinner, Lola realized that the soldiers spoke openly and without discretion. One day some officers spoke about Union plans and strategy on the front porch, thinking they were safe. Lola overheard the officers talking about a surprise attack on the Confederates who were "higher up on the St. Johns on the west side." Still seething about her father being imprisoned, Lola overheard officers discussing the raid that would involve the Union gunboat, the USS *Columbine*. Lola called her sisters Pachita and Eugenia to her. She arranged with her sisters to cover for her while she made her way to Confederate lines to alert them to the Union plans. According to a story recounted in J. L. Underwood's book from 1906, *The Women of the Confederacy*:

> *Stealing softly from the house, she sped to the horse lot, and throwing a saddle on her horse rode for life to the ferry, a mile distant; there the ferryman took her horse, and gave her a boat she rowed herself across the St. Johns, met one Confederate picket, who knew her and gave her his horse.*

Lola made her way to Camp Davis, where she asked to meet with Capt. John Jackson Dickinson. She told him that on Sunday, the Yankees planned on ascending St. Johns to trap the Confederates. They would also be sending out foraging parties. After explaining the whole situation to the captain, she took the picket's horse and exited the camp to the ferry. She left the horse with the Confederate picket who had loaned her his horse. Once across the river, she mounted her horse, arriving back at home just in time for dinner. Her sisters had done an excellent job covering for her, and she was never missed.

Meanwhile, the officers at the Sanchez home had no idea that while they ate, Captain Dickinson had left Camp Davis with Confederate soldiers to lay a trap for the unsuspecting Union soldiers. They would cross the St. Johns to the east side to wait. This battle would become known as the Battle of Horse Landing. It would make Lola a hero and the Union raid unsuccessful.

The Horse Landing Project in Flordia records that battle took place on May 23, 1864. The Confederate's "2nd Florida Cavalry and a battery from the Milton Light Artillery" disabled and captured the USS *Columbine*, which was moving up the St. John's River to trap the Confederates. They also caught a transport. Many of the Union soldiers were captured or killed. According to some versions of the story, General Chatfield was killed, and Col. William H. Noble, commander of the 17th Connecticut Infantry, was captured. Noble was eventually paroled in April 1865. The Union soldiers did not know they had been tipped off by Sanchez, age sixteen when the war started and by 1864 now twenty. It was a humiliating defeat for the Union to lose their gunboat. Rear Adm. John A. Dahlgren summed up the loss:

> *The loss of the Columbine will be felt most inconveniently; her draft was only 5 or 6 feet, and having only two such steamers, the service of which are needed elsewhere, can not replace her.*

After the Battle of Horse Landing, a "pontoon was captured and renamed 'The Three Sisters'" in compliment to these brave young women. The three sisters had one more mission to fulfill. They wanted to have their father released from the St. Augustine jail. He was not a young man but in his fifties, in ill health and disabled. Pachita went by herself to St. Augustine after being permitted to travel by a Union officer and was able to secure his release.

Once the war concluded, Lola married Confederate soldier Emanuel Lopez on June 1, 1868. Her sister Eugenia also married a local Confederate soldier. Panchita moved from Florida to South Carolina after marrying John R. Miot, a captain in the Confederate army. After the war through the US Census in 1880, Lola and Emanuel were farmers, and they had ten children in fourteen years. She would pass away on October 10, 1895, and would be buried in the family plot in All Souls Parish Catholic Cemetery in Palatka, Florida. Her husband would live until 1907 and would be buried in the same cemetery.

Chapter Eight

Unfinished Lives, Part I

WHAT THESE YOUNG SOLDIERS EXPERIENCED WAS HORRIFIC. IT HAS been estimated that over two hundred thousand soldiers below the age of eighteen enlisted in the Confederate and Union armies combined. *Kids in the Civil War*, a documentary featured on PBS, summed it up best, saying many child soldiers survived the war, but not unscathed. They were shot at, wounded, and "listened as wounded men pleaded for their mothers, for a drink of water, or for death to come." Many children soldiers survived, but still others never married, had children, or even saw their loved ones again. They left unfinished lives. Some died "gloriously" in a battle, dubbed heroes if someone saw their heroic act or remembered them. Others died quietly in prison camps or of diseases.

Many child soldiers began their service as drummer boys. Their reasons for enlisting were similar to many of the men who enlisted in the very same regiments. Some joined for excitement or adventure. Still others yearned to leave abusive homes or be near family members such as older brothers and fathers. A few were orphans who had no one, and the potential, if they were lucky, to collect a steady income which appealed to them. If parents in the home could not initially be coaxed to let their children leave for war, they were appeased by officers who told them as drummer boys, they were seen as noncombatants. When the nation was still mainly agrarian, the loss of a child meant the loss of labor and sometimes income if they worked in a factory. Finally, some children were allowed to enlist because of sign-on bonuses and monthly wages.

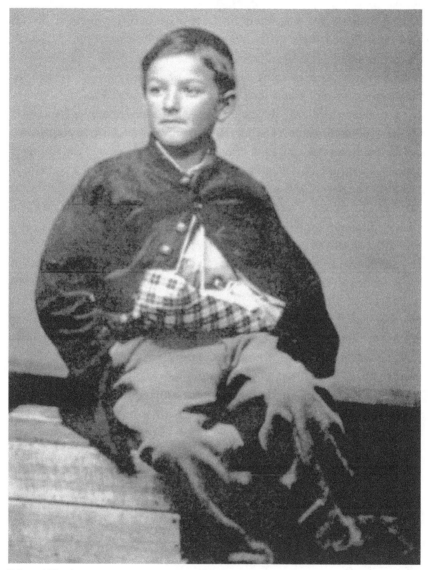

Edward Black

Their age did not necessarily shelter them from danger because, after all, war is dangerous. Sometimes, these young enlistees were forced to take up muskets, act as couriers, or assist in evacuating wounded. Sometimes this placed them at the wrong place at the right time. Although the earlier chapters concentrated on the survivors of the war, who were grievously wounded in some cases, some of these boy soldiers died. In this chapter, we will take a look at their tragically brief lives.

For some "soldiers," it was the first time they had ever handled a musket. In some instances guns were not up to standards and could be unsafe. Such was the case for Clarence D. McKenzie, one of the youngest casualties of the Civil War. He was not a combat death, but merely an accident. The *Brooklyn Eagle*, on June 15, 1861, recounted the story of his demise. The thirteen-year-old drummer boy enlisted in the 13th New York Regiment Company D. Clarence served alongside his brother, who was also, because of his age, a drummer boy.

Soldiers and even drummer boys needed to practice the manual of arms. Although they were probably not supposed to practice in barracks, it did happen. Battles were so chaotic that sometimes the only thing that could be heard over the roar of battles was a drum or a bugle. Soldiers needed to know the correct way to play orders on these instruments. Drilling was no different. Knowing the proper way to drill was a step in training that could ultimately save your life.

While practicing in the barracks at Annapolis on June 11, 1861, Clarence practiced the manual of arms with a fellow soldier. Several newspapers, including the *Brooklyn Eagle* on June 15, 1861, said that when it came to "a charge bayonets his [soldier,] hand struck the hammer of his piece, forcing it down—although he says it was half-cocked and discharging it." Half-cock was the safety on a musket. Soldiers as far back as the American Revolution knew that the springs sometimes became fatigued over time. Sometimes the spring became so weakened that it allowed the musket to go off at half-cock. Hence, the origin of the expression, "go off half-cocked."

Within an instant, the musket ball entered Clarence's back, exiting through his stomach. It continued on its trajectory after leaving the boy's body, ricocheting off the barracks' brick wall. It splintered parts of the brick. Hearing a shot coming from the barracks, fellow soldiers ran toward the noise, arriving to see Clarence's crumpled body on the ground. A few of the men cradled the boy as they took him to the camp hospital. As he probed the wound, the surgeon realized there was nothing he could do; he looked up and declared the injury was too severe for him to do anything more for the child. Clarence lived in agony for roughly two hours. Those who were with him remembered that his mental faculties were present. However, when he tried to speak, he was unable to utter a word.

There was an outpouring of emotion for such a young casualty from fellow soldiers and the nation. Newspapers reported that some three thousand people attended his funeral. Incredibly emotional for the public was the story of his beloved pet terrier. When the boy's body was brought home, the dog would not leave his master, remaining on guard next to Clarence's coffin. In a pamphlet written as a memorial to the fallen child soldier, Rev. Thomas C. Strong wrote that "The funeral cortege set out from the residence of the deceased's parents, on Liberty Street, between three and four o'clock and proceeded down Concord Street to St. John's Church. . . ." The Rev. Dr. Guion conducted the service.

After the funeral, the coffin was opened for a final viewing, allowing those present to say one more goodbye. His classmates from Public School No. 1 whom he left for the war also filed past the coffin to pay their last respects. Eventually, a funeral procession made its way to Greenwood Cemetery. A reporter recorded that "four drummers rolled the dead march in front of the cortege, and over the open grave, where three rounds of musketry were fired."

Some hours after the interment, a person walked by the new grave. Lying on the newly dug earth, the boy's little terrier appeared to the onlooker as grief-stricken. When people tried to coax him to leave the grave, the little dog refused to leave the gravesite. As the days went on, his beloved dog briefly left to go home and eat. Once finished, he returned to keep vigil over Clarence's grave.

There were soldiers even younger than Clarence who met their end on the battlefield. One died during the bloodiest single day of fighting in the Civil War—Antietam.

The Battle of Antietam or Sharpsburg was fought on September 17, 1862, between forces led by Union general George B. McClellan and Confederate general Robert E. Lee. Combined casualties for both sides were staggering at over twenty-two thousand. During the Confederate invasion of the North, Charlie King from Westchester, Pennsylvania, was a mere twelve and a half years old. He was the oldest of eight children, born in April 1849. King was the son of Pennel and Adaline King. His father had also decided to join the Union army. Charlie joined on September 12, 1861, under Capt. Benjamin H. Sweney in Company F of the 49th Pennsylvania Regiment. Pennel King was not happy that his son wanted to join the army, but when the recruiting officer reassured him that his son would be out of harm's way, the father relented. He was enlisted as a drummer and still later became a drum major for the company. What is interesting to note is that his age on the muster roll is "18." Charlie was mustered into service on the 25th of the same month and year in Harrisburg, Pennsylvania. He would be paid by January 1, 1862.

During the Battle of Antietam, Charlie was in the "East Woods near the Miller Cornfield." A Confederate artillery shell exploded, spraying shrapnel into the men. Charlie was near the explosion, which sent a piece of shrapnel through the boy's body. In Westbrook's *History of the 49th Pennsylvania*, he related that after a piece of shrapnel pierced Charlie, he collapsed into the arms of H. H. Bowles of the 6th Maine Regiment. The lifeless body of Charlie King was evacuated to a field hospital where he died from his wounds three days later. His father was summoned to his son. Where he is buried is not known for sure. It is open to conjecture even whether his father made it in time to see his son die or if he took Charlie's body back home.

Sometimes soldiers moving across a battlefield encountered child soldiers who had been killed or wounded. In Emmy E. Werner's book *Reluctant Witnesses*, she quotes a Union musician, John A. Cockerill, who was only sixteen, who found such an encounter traumatic, even if it was the body of a Confederate.

I passed . . . the corpse of a beautiful boy in gray who lay with his blond curls scattered about his face and his hand folded peacefully

across his breast. He was clad in a bright and neat uniform, well gar-
nished with gold, which seemed to tell the story of a loving mother and
sisters who had sent their household pet to the field of war. His neat
little hat lying beside him bore the number of a Georgia regiment. . . .
He was about my age. . . . At the sight of the poor boy's corpse, I burst
into a regular boohoo and started on.

Rashio Crane was fifteen years old when he joined the 7th Wisconsin Infantry. He was mustered in as a private in Company D. His first real taste of battle was during the Wilderness Campaign. Lasting from May 5 to May 7, 1864, this campaign was an attack by General Grant on the Army of Northern Virginia to bring the war to a close. Rashio was the drummer. However, sometimes the wounded became so overwhelming that drummers were asked to help evacuate the casualties. In this campaign, the Union lost around seventeen thousand soldiers. Rashio was helping a wounded comrade when Confederates captured him.

He was born in Mt. Pleasant, Racine County, Wisconsin, on November 13, 1848, and enlisted on February 2, 1864. Probably because his struggling family needed the steady income because his father had died, his mother allowed her sons to join the army. In theory, she would not have to worry about feeding them either.

Rashio had only been in the army for five months when he was captured. He was sent to the notorious hellhole Andersonville Prison in Georgia. The conditions in prison were horrible. With so many soldiers, unsanitary conditions, and little food, dysentery ran rampant throughout the camp. Rashio contracted it, and with the little medical attention given the prisoners, he died on July 23, 1864. His remains were interred in what later became the Andersonville National Cemetery. A year later, his mother, Mary A. Crane, applied for a pension in her late son's name. She applied on April 15, 1865, and it was approved.

Disease caused more death than actual fighting. Since the dawn of armies, dysentery had been a major killer. This ailment causing painful cramps, bloody diarrhea, and dehydration took the lives of many soldiers, as unsanitary conditions made it endemic to large armies. Many times, the cure was worse than the ailment. Medicines used could cause teeth to fall out or slowly poison the victim. It was a constant battle for organizations like the Sanitary Commission to enforce bathing and washing clothing. In many instances, privies were too close to sources of drinking water, which became contaminated. Finally, food that was heavy on bread and meat wreaked havoc on men's stomachs. Exacerbating the situation, sometimes the food was borderline spoiled or fried to make it taste better. For many of the soldiers, vegetables could not be added in significant quantities. Disease-carrying mosquitoes were another constant source of misery, prevalent when soldiers camped near water. Malaria is still a dreaded disease carried by mosquitoes. It fell many soldiers in the field, such as young Charles C. Taylor from Upstate New York.

Taylor was born in Washington County, New York, on November 17, 1848, to Thomas and Louisa Taylor. He enlisted in Plattsburgh in the Union army's 175th New York Infantry Regiment as a private. Taylor signed on for one year and was supposed to be discharged in 1865. He stood at 5'4", and his enlistment papers listed him as having blue eyes, brown hair, and a light complexion. He enlisted on September 13, 1864. Why Charles decided to join is not known, but the fact that his father, who Charles resembled, had also enlisted might have been a factor. Thomas Taylor, at thirty-seven years of age, joined the 153rd New York State Infantry Company K on September 9, 1862. He signed on for three years. Thomas was mustered in as a private on October 18, 1862. He would be discharged for a disability on March 31, 1865.

Charles never reached the end of his year-long commitment. Two months later, in York, Virginia (some records list York, Pennsylvania), he contracted malaria. When he became stricken with the illness, he was sent to a local hospital to recover. Charles did not recover; he died six days shy of his sixteenth birthday. The cause of his death was described as a congestive fever, which was a direct result of a complication of malaria. His family brought him home, where he was buried in Sunnyside Cemetery. Across the bottom of the stone is the epitaph, "in defense of his country."

We must remember that these children were witnessing events that were part of an adult war. Doctors labeled war's adverse psychological effects with terms like nostalgia, melancholy, heavy heart, neuralgia, and even cowardice. Later, in World War I the term *shell-shocked* would be used, and still later *post-traumatic stress disorder* (PTSD). Tony Horwitz, in *Smithsonian Magazine*, wrote that "the Civil War killed and injured over a million Americans, roughly a third of all those who served, this grim tally, however, doesn't include the conflict's psychic wounds." Edward Black has the dubious distinction of being the youngest soldier on both sides of the conflict who had his life cut short by the war's scars.

Black was born on May 30, 1853, in Hagerstown, Indiana. His family relocated shortly after his birth to Indianapolis. He was the son of George A. and Lydia Black. When just eight years old, on July 24, 1861, Edward enlisted in the 21st Indiana Infantry as a musician in Company L. Eventually, because of his youth or a wound, he was sent home by August 16, 1862, only to reenlist with his father who was a first lieutenant in Company L.

The same year, 1862, he was captured by the Confederate army during the Battle of Baton Rouge on August 5, 1862. Once captured, he was confined to Ship Island in the Gulf of Mexico. When federal troops retook Baton Rouge on August 20, 1862, Black was freed. Triumphantly, he entered Baton Rouge with his fellow soldiers. Once again, he was discharged in August 1862 in Baltimore for a disability. His service record does not state the cause of the disability. Another contributing reason for his discharge was because President Lincoln had ordered drummer boys to be discharged from the army. Drummer boys were frequently minors, and because they led the troops into battles often, they became targets.

Shortly after being released as a prisoner of war and discharged from the Union army, Edward Black reenlisted in February 1863, with his old unit. However, his old company had been reorganized into the 1st Indiana Heavy Artillery Regiment. While with this regiment, a Confederate shell exploded close to Edward, shattering his left arm and hand. According to one source, Edward Black was not discharged until 1866, when he was well enough to leave the hospital.

When he arrived home, he went about trying to find work. Edward found work as a painter while living with his parents. There are no surviving records at that point to speak to how well he integrated back into society. Still a young boy, he undoubtedly suffered as some did from the horrible memories of the war. Newspapers reported that he died on June 30, 1872, at 7:00 p.m. at his parents' home. He was only nineteen years of age. Many who knew him believed that the cause of his death at such a young age was his injury and the trauma inflicted during the war, although the obituary in the *Indianapolis Evening News* for July 1 listed Scrofula, a tuberculosis-related condition, as the cause of death.

His family buried him in the Crown Hill Cemetery, in Indianapolis, Indiana. Lydia, his mother, applied for her son's pension on January 30, 1888. She did collect a widow's pension when her husband died in 1889.

Edwin Francis Jemison's face stares back at us from 150 years in the past, just sixteen years old with boyish looks that made him look more like fourteen or fifteen. His gaze in his new Confederate uniform has come to represent the hundreds of thousands of child soldiers who enlisted in both the Blue and the Gray. His death has come to represent the tragedy of the Civil War. A little over a year after he passed, the *Southern Recorder* for August 5, 1863, carried news of his death. He was a member of the 2nd Infantry Regiment of Louisiana Volunteers.

Jemison was born on December 1, 1844, in Milledgeville, Georgia. He was one of five sons of Robert Jemison and Sarah Caroline Stubb (Jemison), who had married in 1841. Edward was their second-oldest son, born to a well-off family. His father was a landowner, lawyer, as well as a newspaper editor. In 1850, his worth in real estate alone was $4,000. He listed himself in 1850 as a farmer.

By the birth of their third son Samuel Hunter Jemison, the family had relocated to Jackson, Louisiana, where the family lived at the out-break of the Civil War. Louisiana seceded from the United States on January 26, 1861, joining the Confederate States of America. That spring, Edwin enlisted as a private on May 11, 1861, in Company B, known as Moore's Guards. The company belonged to the 2nd Regiment of the Louisiana Infantry. He was signed on at Camp Walker in New Orleans by Capt. J. M. Galt.

His regiment was ordered to Virginia, where they were assigned to the Department of Peninsula. They were sent to Richmond, Virginia, and then to Yorktown and eventually to Williamsburg, Virginia. Certainly, Private Jemison was in Williamsburg, because the muster roll for his company noted that he was sick in Williamsburg in December 1861. According to the company muster roll, he was off the ill list for January and February 1862. The following month Maj. Gen. George F. McClellan, known to his men as "Little Mac," commenced his offensive known as the Peninsula Campaign. During this campaign, Jemison switched companies within his regiment. He switched by May 1862 to Company C, known as the Pelican Greys.

Private Jemison tasted his first real combat during this campaign. He would be involved in a skirmish at Lee's Mill on April 16, 1862, when attacked. It was when the Army of the Potomac was in full retreat and occupying Malvern Hill that he would be in his first massive battle. Unfortunately, it would also be his last battle. It was the final battle of the Seven Days Battles, which also ended McClellan's Peninsula Campaign. McClellan's goal was to conquer the capital of the Confederacy, Richmond.

Battlefield Trust, which seeks to preserve Civil War battlefields, states that "On July 1, 1862, the retreating Army of the Potomac reached the James River after six days of fighting outside of Richmond. Confident in support of nearby navy gunboats, Maj. Gen. George McClellan's men occupied Malvern Hill on the north bank of the river. McClellan ordered the hilltop fortified with artillery batteries to cover the open fields that fronted the hill, and arranged his infantry with the V Corps on the west slope and the III and IV Corps on the eastern side with a strong reserve in the rear." General Robert E. Lee ordered his troops to attack the defended position by the afternoon of July 1, 1862. According to the *Southern Recorder* for August 5, 1862, "Edwin Francis Jemison, a member of the 2d Regiment Louisiana Volunteers, fell in the battle of Malvern Hill, on the 1st July, 1862, aged seventeen years and seven months." The obituary continued, "He was stricken down in the front rank without a struggle yielded up his young life."

With his death, how he died became a subject of debate. Some said a cannonball took off the young man's head to the horror of those around him. His brother, Samuel, who died in 1887, also stated that this was the way his brother died. However, some believe he was shot down. Where his remains were laid to rest has also been a subject of debate. His obituary stated, "buried by loving hands, on the battlefield near Richmond." However, some believe he was reinterred in Memory Hill Cemetery in Milledgeville, Georgia, where he was born. An obelisk is over the alleged grave shared by a brother who died before him. Edwin's grave was erected after the Civil War when organizations wanted to give the soldiers proper burials. Some believe that this is what happened with the grave of Pvt. Edwin Francis Jemison.

Benjamin R. Knox came from a large family in Ohio. The Civil War would be particularly brutal for the Knox family. They sacrificed two of their sons to preserve the Union, including their eighteen-year-old Benjamin, in 1864. Knox was born in 1846 according to the 1850 US Census. During this census year, the family lived in Miller, located in Knox County, Ohio He was the son of Henry and Alzina Knox. His father and mother were both born in New York and moved west into Ohio. In 1850, his father was listed as a tavern keeper. By 1860, the year of Benjamin's fourteenth birthday, he was still living in Knox County, Ohio. Benjamin's father was listed as a wagoner, and there were now ten family members sharing the home.

When the war started, Benjamin enlisted on November 20, 1861, as a private. He was assigned to one company and then later was reassigned to the 20th Ohio Infantry Company H. The 20th Ohio had been organized at Columbus, Ohio, from August 19 to September 21, 1861. Afterward they relocated to Camp King near Covington, Kentucky. They were officially mustered in on October 21, 1861. When Benjamin enlisted, he signed on for three years.

The 20th Ohio saw a lot of action. They were on duty at Covington and Newport, Kentucky, until February 11, 1862. By February 14, they were present at the Western Theater's major battles: the attack on Fort Donelson, Shiloh, the Siege of Corinth, and Vicksburg. His three-year enlistment expired, and by July 1864, he enlisted again for another three years in time for Sherman's Atlanta Campaign. He was listed at age eighteen as a veteran.

Private Knox, from July 22, 1864, until his death, was part of the Siege of Atlanta. The siege was meant to starve Atlanta into submission and surrender. It was shortly after the battle of Ezra Chapel, a Methodist

Church, that a skirmish ensued. Private Knox was in a trench when he was shot and mortally wounded. He was evacuated to a hospital where he died on August 10, 1864, twelve days before Atlanta surrendered. Private Knox was buried in what by 1867 became the Marietta National Cemetery. Initially, according to his burial record, he was buried at the foot of a Spanish oak. Later, it is believed, his body was moved to its present resting spot. In 1879, his mother would apply for her son's pension, which she was granted.

These are but a few of the child soldiers that were killed on both sides of the conflict. Others perished but remain nameless. One such example is the fourteen-year-old Confederate soldier killed by a bayonet at Fort Mahone during the battle of St. Petersburg. He died about a week before the surrender at Appomattox. His picture is commonly used to expose the horror of the Civil War.

These children entered into a new type of warfare. It was what became referred to as a total war, a move toward what we know today as modern warfare. The armies that fought it were unprepared for it, society was unprepared for its destruction, and the medical establishment unprepared for the onslaught of wounded needing care. This war very quickly transformed society. There is no doubt the children who enlisted in the war entered an adult world of carnage, death, misery, and destruction. These wounds would be carried with them for the rest of their lives. Some died directly in the war, and others, like Edward Black, died from its effects.

These seven child soldiers above are but a few of the children who gave their lives in the Civil War.

PART II
WOMEN SOLDIERS OF THE CIVIL WAR

CHAPTER NINE

Albert D. J. Cashier (Jennie Hodgers)

ON OCTOBER 12, 1915, ALBERT D. J. CASHIER'S REMAINS LAY IN A plain coffin in Angevine Undertaking in East Moline, Illinois, clothed in the cherished uniform he wore for three years while fighting with the 95th Illinois Volunteer Infantry in the Civil War. Those members of the local Grand Army of the Republic's Graham Post met at their hall at 1:00 p.m. to make their way over to the funeral, which started at 2:30 p.m. After the funeral, a procession left East Moline at 3:35 p.m. traveling along the Milwaukee Road to the Sunny Slope Cemetery in Saunemin, Illinois. Two priests conducted a short service for the soldier who was called "Al" by his comrades. The coffin was then lowered into the ground. Most of the soldiers present that day knew of the secret that Albert kept for the first six decades of his life. They did not much care that one of the bravest men they ever knew was born Jennie Hodgers.

In the book *The Senate's Civil War*, when Fort Sumter surrendered on April 13, 1861, "President Lincoln issued a proclamation on April 15 calling upon Congress to convene an emergency session on July 4. He also called for 75,000 troops to protect the seat of government and suppress the rebellion—although they were asked to serve for only 90 days." The president called for an additional forty-three thousand troops to volunteer the following month. By the end of the summer of 1862, Lincoln called for three hundred thousand volunteers. These volunteers signed on for three years.

Illinois Adjutant General Jasper N. Reece wrote: "[Cashier's] regiment was organized at Camp Fuller, Rockford, Illinois, by Colonel

Lawrence S. Church, and was mustered into the United States service September 4, 1862. Seven companies were recruited from McHenry County and three from Boone County."

Albert Cashier belonged to Company G. He enlisted on August 6, 1862, and was mustered into the regular army on September 4, 1862, by officers Thomas Humphrey and Elliott N. Bush. They recorded his age as nineteen, and at 5'3" in height, the shortest in the regiment. Al had amber hair, blue eyes, and a light complexion, and some remembered

Woman Soldier in 95th Ill.

ALBERT D. J. CASHIER
OF
COMPANY G, 95TH ILLINOIS REGIMENT

Photographed November, 1864

ALBERT D. J. CASHIER
OF
COMPANY G, 95TH ILLINOIS REGIMENT

Photographed July, 1913

Albert D. J. Cashier pictured while in the army and in his later years
COURTESY OF THE ABRAHAM LINCOLN PRESIDENTIAL LIBRARY & MUSEUM

"that he had smallpox at some time, because when he entered the service, his face was quite pitted." Albert, an unmarried farmer, claimed to be initially from New York City, drifting out west. Some soldiers remembered him frequently smoking a pipe. When he did speak they remembered a thick Irish brogue. No one recalled a comprehensive physical examination by doctors, at least none that required you to strip, which to many explained how Private Cashier eluded detection.

Albert remained aloof and distant from the soldiers around him to guard his secret carefully. When it came to camp life, fellow inductees noted that he did not participate in any of the regular activities such as sports or horsing around. Some men suspected he might be what they referred to as a "half and half" because no one ever saw him bathe or unclothed, but other soldiers washed erratically. However, when there was a job to do, Albert got it done no matter the danger. No one ever questioned his almost reckless bravery. Still, another soldier, named Joy H. Saxton, recalled, "he seemed to be able to do as much work as anyone in the camp . . . he signed his name by mark. I think his mind was alright, and he was not simple in anyway."

A lot of what we know about the 95th and Albert Cashier comes from two sources. The first source is the 95th's Regimental History. Also, there is a detailed account of a soldier's life in the Civil War Letters of Sgt. Onley Andrus, edited by Fred Albert Shannon. Sergeant Andrus was in the 95th with Cashier, but Company C, not Company G. He does not mention Albert in his letters home. His writings are valuable because they shed light on Cashier's role in the Vicksburg Campaign. Still other sources are newspapers, the letters of Pvt. Samuel Pepper, and other accounts after the war by veterans who remembered Al. Samuel Pepper, unlike Andrus, was in the same company as Al.

Pvt. Albert D. J. Cashier left Camp Fuller, after training for some two months, and on November 4, 1862, he arrived in Cairo, Illinois. From Cairo, he moved with the 95th to Columbus, Kentucky, then eventually on to Jackson, Tennessee. The 95th camped at Collierville, Tennessee, arriving there on the 2nd; while there, they were repairing and guarding the railroads that were the Union army's lifeline for moving supplies as well as troops. By January 13, 1863, the 95th went into camp about three miles from Memphis, where they were assigned to Gen. John McArthur's Division, Army of the Tennessee. At this time, the commanding officer of the 95th was Col. Lawrence S. Church, who, because of his health, eventually turned over command to Col. Thomas Humphrey.

Private Cashier's early engagement with the Confederates was during Gen. Ulysses S. Grant's campaign in northern Mississippi between 1862 and 1863. The goal was to capture the Mississippi and split the eastern part of the Confederacy from the western Confederacy, namely Texas, Louisiana, and Arkansas. These states provided valuable supplies for the Confederate war effort. One of the obstacles to Union control of the Mississippi was Vicksburg.

According to Wood, who wrote the regimental history, on January 19, 1863, the 95th Illinois Infantry boarded the steamer *Marie Denning* for the trip to Vicksburg after being placed under the command of Maj. Gen. James B. McPherson. Embarking with the 95th "were the Eleventh Iowa, Eighteenth Wisconsin, and one company of the Second Illinois Artillery." Also, in addition to all the soldiers, the steamer transports contained artillery, wagons, mules, and horses. These transports quickly became cramped spaces. Sometimes men shared the same area as animals. So little room made it necessary for the steamers to stop onshore at night for the men to sleep more comfortably on land. The flotilla of transports numbered about fifteen steamers.

The troop transports arrived on January 25, 1863, at Milliken's Bend, Louisiana, located several miles above a canal under construction by Union soldiers. Sergeant Andrus recorded that the canal was strategically desirable because it provided a channel for Union ships to proceed to a point below Vicksburg, thus permitting an attack from the rear. Albert and his company worked on this canal located at Young's Point, Louisiana. Soldiers remembered the back-breaking labor involved in the construction dug mostly by hand. Cashier and other soldiers were assigned day and night shifts.

Albert and his regiment were later sent to Lake Providence, Louisiana, to commence construction on another canal. When both canals were completed, General Grant hoped that the water flooding in from both the Mississippi River and Lake Providence would allow steamer transports to pass through. The costly project was quickly deemed a failure because the channels proved too shallow for the larger Union vessels. However, all was not lost because agricultural lands were inundated by water, denying the Confederate army valuable food and fodder for their horses.

Wood writes that the hard work in the hostile environment, to men not accustomed to it, took its toll on their health. Sunstroke, exhaustion, dysentery, fevers, and malaria sent countless soldiers to their deaths or the hospital. Andrus penned, "this is not a very healthy country even at this season of the year." The diet of the men was also lacking. It consisted of "Hog & Hard Bread & Coffee and Tea." Some soldiers chose not to eat meat because of taste or that it was borderline spoiled. Andrus pointed out that he did not like eating "hog," which left him with less variety. Much later in life, Cashier described that he ate a lot of meat during his time in the Civil War, and after he left, not so much.

A lot of the work and other "thankless" duties left the soldiers of the 95th aching for battle. So far, Cashier and his fellow soldiers had not "seen the elephant," a period phrase for seeing combat. Andrus wrote to his wife Mary, on April 26, that she should not worry about him going into danger because he did not think they will be going into battle, "and if we should go into a fight, I don't calculate to get killed." Andrus wrote again on May 9, 1863, about the lack of action, referring to his regiment as "the bold Bloodless 95th."

Shannon, the editor of the Andrus letters, writes that the 95th, in the next two weeks, not only saw the elephant but, like many soldiers, probably wished not to see it again. As far as Sergeant Andrus, once they started to see more and more action, he complained that the commanding officer, Colonel Humphrey, wanted to earn a general's star. If the men misbehaved, he explained to his wife, it was because they knew the plan of the colonel, not due to lack of courage.

They finally tasted battle on May 19, 1863, when Grant's Canal was deemed a failure, and it was decided to launch a full attack on Vicksburg. Wood writes, "a charge was ordered along our whole lines upon the enemy's works, to take place at two o clock in the afternoon, and at the appointed hour the furious onset commenced. The 95th held an important position in the brigade during this memorable charge, and, led forward by its gallant colonel, advanced under a galling fire to a ridge within one hundred yards of the rebel works, and held the position during the remainder of the day." Colonel Humphrey was shot in the foot but remained in command of his 95th. Vicksburg, to Grant's dismay, held out against the attack. Colonel Humphrey received orders to withdraw at nightfall, which he did. In his article for the *Illinois Historical Journal*, Rodney O. Davis related a quote from an interview of Lt. C. W. Ives originally published on May 30, 1923, in the *Omaha Bee*:

> *I remember one time when our column got cut off from the rest of the company because we were too outnumbered to advance. There was a place where three dead trees piled one on top of another formed a sort of barricade. The rebels got down out of sight. "Al" hopped on the top of the log and called "Hey! You darn rebels, why don't you get up where we see you?"*

Ives remembered telling Cashier to get down because he was sure to get killed. Some six decades later, he shook his head, wondering how so many bullets missed the private. He also recalled that at another battle Private Cashier had climbed a tall tree to rehang a Union flag to a limb where a Rebel had shot it down. On May 22, a Rebel fortification still stood before Cashier, and Grant wanted it taken.

> *General Grant, with his characteristic perseverance, ordered the assault to be renewed on the 22nd of May, with the intention, if possible, of breaking through the enemy's line at certain points, then of heavily reinforcing the successful assaulting column, with the hope and prospect of thus carrying the day. At ten o'clock A.M., on the 22nd, the charge began again furiously. The Ninety-fifth, on this occasion, also gained an advance position on the crest of the ridge near the enemy's works, encountering one of the most sweeping and destructive fires to which troops were ever exposed. . . .*

Sergeant Andrus's words took on a prophetic sentiment when in April, he wrote, "by the shape of matters & things are taking I think that there is no doubt but that Vicksburg will be taken but not without a great loss of life." Captain Manzer of Company C, and Capt. Gabriel E. Cornwell, of Company K, were both killed; Maj. William Avery, Capt. Edward J. Cook of Company D, Lt. Otis H. Smith of Company C, Lt. James E. Sponable of Company A, and Lt. Converse Pierce of Company I, were wounded quite severely. The 95th's history lists the total killed at 25 with 124 injured and ten presumed captured.

When it became apparent that this attack would also prove unsuccessful, the Union troops and the 95th settled into what became known as the Siege of Vicksburg. Mary Catherine Lannon, who wrote the dissertation *Albert D. J. Cashier and the Ninety-Fifth Illinois Infantry (1844–1915)*, citing an Illinois newspaper, recorded that during the siege Albert volunteered for a skirmish expedition probing for weaknesses in the Confederate lines. The Rebels captured Cashier. He eventually escaped when he overpowered a sentry, securing an officer's horse and returning to the safety of the Union lines.

During the siege, it is believed that water supplies became contaminated. Albert ingested some of this water and started to suffer from what he termed "chronic diarrhea." He suffered from this condition for the rest of his life. It became enough of a problem for Private Cashier that an officer had him seek relief from the regimental doctor. Albert must have felt intense anxiety because where there were doctors there was the chance of being told to undress. Even when ill with dysentery, he managed to stay out of the regimental hospital, where he might have been required to bathe.

After a siege lasting more than forty days, the Rebels surrendered Vicksburg on July 3, 1863. On Independence Day 1863, "the 95th Illinois was among the first regiments to enter Vicksburg." Although it is sometimes written that Cashier entered the fallen fortress on July 4, that might not be true because he was so gripped with dysentery. There is no mention if he stayed back or marched.

Shortly after the fall of Vicksburg, Port Hudson, Louisiana, fell on July 9, 1863. The entire Mississippi lay in the hands of the Union. By July 12, 1863, Gen. Thomas E. G. Ransom's Brigade, of which the 95th was now included, boarded steamers for Natchez, Mississippi, arriving one day later. They disembarked without ever firing a shot. Shannon wrote, "their purpose was to put down Confederate opposition, pacify inhabitants and capture military stores that might be of benefit to the Confederate armies." Cashier, if we believe Onley's letter home, lived like a king while quartered in Natchez. The troops ate fresh fruit, vegetables, and meat. Leaves home were granted for some of the soldiers. There was no mention in surviving records or local newspapers of Cashier going on home leave. Unfortunately, over the next year, the war exacted an act of vengeance on the 95th. Some soldiers could not have known that they were seeing their loved ones for the last time when on leave. Many of the men whom Cashier fought alongside perished in the coming year.

In October 1863, the 95th returned to Vicksburg, where they remained until February 1864, mainly assigned picket duty. They briefly joined Major General Sherman on the Meridian Expedition in February 1864 but did not see combat. In March of 1864, the Red River Campaign started, and they were to meet Maj. Gen. Nathaniel Banks at the mouth of the Red River. Its goal was to occupy Shreveport, Louisiana, which was the headquarters for the Army of the Trans-Mississippi. Once secured, the Union hoped to use Shreveport to launch an invasion of Texas.

Cashier, in the brigade of Col. Lyman Ward of the 14th Wisconsin Infantry, tasted success with the destruction of Fort DeRussy on March 14, 1864, which stood in the way of the military objective. Cashier and the 95th continued to march to central Louisiana. The battles of Pleasant Hill and Mansfield brought to an end the campaign that Major General Sherman called "one damn blunder from beginning to end." Although they did not participate in the Red River Campaign's major battles, the 95th did see fighting in the battle of Yellow Bayou on May 18, 1864, while they retreated toward the mouth of the Red River.

The 95th was ordered to Memphis in May 1864. Cashier left Memphis on June 1st aboard the Memphis and Charleston Railroad with the 81st and 113th Illinois Infantry. They eventually arrived on June 9, 1864, at Ripley, Mississippi. On June 10, 1864, Brig. Gen. Samuel Davis Sturgis and his cavalry were involved in protecting the railroad lines that resupplied Major General Sherman on his Atlanta Campaign. Sturgis engaged Maj. Gen. Nathan Bedford Forrest when he was miles ahead of his infantry support. The two generals clashed at Brice's Crossroad on June 10, 1864, in a battle also known as the Battle of Guntown. Cashier and his comrades were marching through some of the most punishing heat that the South could throw at them on their way to assist Sturgis. When they arrived at Guntown, they were in no condition to support the cavalry.

Early in the battle, Colonel Humphrey fell mortally wounded. Capt. William H. Stewart of Company F took over the command, but was carried from the field after being shot through both legs. Cashier's company captain, E. N. Bush, also fell. Finally, Captain Schellenger of Company K took over the command of the 95th. After holding their line for hours, they eventually retreated to Memphis. They were severely beaten, out of ammunition, with none on the way. You could follow their retreat as many fleeing soldiers discarded most of their supplies to hasten their flight. According to the regimental history, "the regiment never before experienced such a disaster as had recently overwhelmed it . . . It only performed light duties, and was allowed a few weeks to recover from the severe shock. . . ."

Once rested and recovered from the shock of Guntown, Wales in another regimental history recorded, "Preparations were now being made for the movement of troops down the Mississippi and up the White River, for operations in Arkansas. On August 3, 1864, the 95th embarked on the steamer *White Cloud* at Memphis and arrived at St. Charles, Arkansas, on the 5th. Company K was detached from the regiment at the mouth of White River, and assigned to garrison that post." The 95th remained at St. Charles until September 1; according to regimental histories, they stayed there on picket duty and building fortifications. They eventually moved upriver looking for Confederate major general Sterling Price's troops threatening to invade Missouri. Cashier and his regiment marched from Arkansas into Missouri, marching some three hundred miles. The shoes they wore were not quality, and by the time they arrived, most soldiers developed holes in the soles. By October 7, 1864, they were transported to Sedalia, Missouri, arriving there on October 16, where they guarded the Missouri-Pacific Railroad. They eventually continued to Benton Barracks in Missouri. After a short time of rest, the regiment helped in defeating General J. B. Hood and pursuing the remnants of his defeated army.

By January 8, 1865, Cashier was busy helping construct winter quarters in Eastport, Mississippi, only to be called out six days later to hunt guerrillas at Corinth, Mississippi. By January 21, 1865, they were sent back to winter quarters. A ration shortage strained the soldiers; Albert was reduced to eating cornbread and popcorn. Some men wrote that next they would be consuming the horse's hay. It was here that Pepper wrote to his wife that he went into business with Cashier washing the clothing of the other soldiers. Friction between Cashier and Pepper came to a head when Cashier did not collect the debt owed them. He also spoke about how impossible Cashier was to share a tent with because he hogged the middle where it was warm instead of rotating, so all had a chance to be warm in the center. Instead, Cashier kept Pepper and another soldier on the sides of the tent, where they froze all night. The men Cashier bunked with nicknamed him "Chubs" (why is not stated).

The war continued to move toward its conclusion, especially after the capture of Mobile on February 6, 1865. Cashier and the 95th would be sent for garrison duty in Opelika, Alabama, a railroad town. While there, Samuel Pepper wrote a letter home to his wife on June 18, 1865, in which he discussed Albert D. J. Cashier in less than flattering terms and his frustration with his use of "dirty talk." Pepper also yearned for home and assured his wife that he hoped to be heading home soon since the war was over. He wanted to rest and, most of all, was tired of eating government rations.

After their garrison duty ended, the 95th went to Montgomery, Alabama, in July, and finally, in August, back to Vicksburg. Cashier and his comrades expected to be mustered out with the rest of the original 95th, but instead, orders arrived to board the steamer *Molly Able* for St. Louis, where they arrived on August 10, 1865. The 95th continued to Springfield, Illinois, where Albert and the rest of the original 95th were finally mustered out on August 17, 1865. However, to their dismay, the soldiers, including Albert, had to continue to wait four more days for back pay the government owed to them. On August 21, 1865, after traveling some ten thousand miles, Pvt. Albert D. J. Cashier was a civilian.

After the war, it becomes challenging to piece together Cashier's whereabouts. It appears that he liked it this way for many reasons. Most importantly, he wanted to keep it a secret that he was actually a woman. Who knows how society would deal with this issue? Apart from his gender identity, it also seems apparent that the Civil War's horrific nature affected his general mental health. His mental health issues manifested, especially later in his life. He already did not trust people because of his "secret." However, Albert also feared that people were trying to do him harm, most notably robbing him. Some other peculiar behaviors became apparent to local citizens who became acquainted with him. They generally accepted his quirks.

When trying to piece together his whereabouts, one of the best sources is Mary Catherine Lannon's mammoth thesis on Albert D. J. Cashier. She grew up in Saunemin, where her family, as well as neighbors, knew him well. She conducted a lot of research as well as oral histories. It must be pointed out that a certain amount is anecdotal. Some of the information that her thesis contains only appears in her writings.

According to Cashier's 1907 petition for a pension, he stated that after the war, he spent time in Kankakee, Illinois, in 1865. The following year he moved to Pontiac and then to Belvidere in 1865, again he went back to Pontiac in 1868, and finally where he would live until 1913, Saunemin, in 1869. Robert D. Hannah, a Civil War veteran who served with Albert, believed that Cashier was in Belvidere, Illinois, in 1866. He remembered seeing him frequently about town. It was here that Cashier worked for a nursery business that fellow soldier Samuel Pepper had started, the same individual who wrote so disparagingly about Cashier. Robert Horan, also a member of Company G, stated, "after his discharge he came here to Belvidere and stayed here until the following spring," which would make it 1866.

Albert lived in Saunemin by 1869 where he worked for Joshua Chesebro doing odd jobs and herding his cattle. Anah Chesebro stated, "the first I remember Albert Cashier was when he came to my parents about 45 years ago." She said this in 1914, which would make Albert's arrival in 1869. She continued, "He really considered our family his home from that time. For years he herded cattle on the prairie for my father."

Her sister Nettie recalled that Albert "was living in a little house near us and would often come to our house for his meals just as he had been in the habit of doing when he lived with us."

Lannon, who interviewed neighbors and family members who knew Cashier, wrote that eventually, Cashier left the Chesebro farm and moved into town. The work might have been too much for him. The health of many soldiers was forever affected by the experiences of army life. Marching in all kinds of weather, irregular diets, and exhaustion took their toll, especially later in life.

When he relocated to town, he worked at the Cording's Hardware Store. Albert worked as a janitor and did odd jobs for Cording. In exchange, the Cording family allowed him to sleep on the floor of the store. Family members told newspapers and still later, Lannon, that Albert frequently took meals with the family. It is here that neighbors remembered some of his quirky behaviors. Maybe as a sign of what today would be called PTSD, Albert became preoccupied with people doing him harm. It was because of this that he insisted on multiple door locks where he slept, as reported in the *Daily Pantagraph* on June 28, 1962. Sometimes after some time with the same locks, he changed them out for newer locks in case someone figured out how to open them.

Saunemin, a small town, allowed the Chesebro family to remain close to Cashier. They grew closer to him, and to make him more comfortable, the family gave him a small building lot on which they constructed a one-room house for him. His fear of robbers became so consuming he installed five or six locks on the door, again changing them all frequently. When leaving the house for more than a few hours, he would "nail the doors and windows shut." In her interviews with townspeople, Lannon remembered other quirky behaviors that were at times disturbing. She writes that sometimes Cashier made cookies for the local children, and when they were about to eat a cookie, she told them not to because they contained poison.

Mrs. E. R. Smith, a neighbor of Albert's, recalled in a local newspaper that Albert asked some neighbors over for some corn he cooked. When about to eat it, Cashier told them to stop because he had given them the wrong corn. The corn they were about to enjoy was poison and meant to trick the rats. No one believed he was trying to kill anyone. They dismissed it as just Albert being Albert.

In 1890, Albert D. J. Cashier filed his first request for a pension. His lawyer, Oscar F. Avery, who practiced in Pontiac, Illinois, filed the paperwork on the February 17. Albert claimed that he was three-quarters disabled and stated that he was both physically and mentally disabled. His physical disability stemmed from around June 15, 1863, when he "was taken sick with chronic diarrhea and was sick in the camp when the regiment marched into Vicksburg." His community supported his application in a petition that Albert was "entirely alone and destitute and is dependent on the charity of the people for aid and support."

On July 5, 1899, Albert D. J. Cashier was "examined" by a doctor on behalf of the Pension Bureau. The doctor recorded in his pension file that:

originally the diarrhea began in Vicksburg. Cashier told the doctor that it sometimes comes out without any pain. I have not eaten but very little meat since I came home from the army. I live principally on bread and a little tea. I have done but very little work for the last ten years as I am too weak. I get short of breath if I hurry and of late years have done nothing but some very little light work.

The doctor wrote that "the claimant is very nervous and shaky." He weighed a mere ninety-four pounds. There is no evidence that the doctor thoroughly examined Cashier, because he is listed as male on the paperwork generated by the physican. After a prolonged waiting period, the government granted Albert a pension of $8 a month. His retirement money still did not prove adequate, so his neighbors continued to find odd jobs for him. Albert Cashier generated extra cash by taking care of the lamps along the streets where he lived. Cashier also became the church's janitor close to his home.

The Lannon family lived just across the street from Albert. During breakfast with them in January 1904, the Christian Church caught fire at about 8:00 a.m. on a Sunday. Citizens rushed to save the house of worship. Their attempts to extinguish the fire were unsuccessful. Afterwards, several people became enraged with Albert because they believed it was his negligence that started the fire. Locals warned him several times about over-stoking the wood stove, which warmed the church. Instead of watching the fire in the stove, the local newspaper reported that "the janitor was at breakfast."

Cashier's health and financial situation continued to deteriorate. In 1907, he requested an increase in his pension. Albert again was granted an increase on March 13, 1907. His monthly check for his military service swelled to $12. Albert continued to keep his secret from not only the federal government, who did not conduct a physical examination even with pension increases, but also from his community. Then everything changed for Albert in 1910.

Lannon, as well as local newspapers, described Albert as sometimes ill and unable to take care of himself. In 1910, Mrs. P. H. Lannon had a nurse from Chicago living in her house and taking care of an ill daughter. Mrs. Lannon became aware that Cashier was also quite sick. She asked the nurse to check in on the ill Civil War veteran, which she agreed to do. A short time later, the nurse came running from the house, screaming that Albert was not a man.

The Lannon family calmed her down. They managed to get the nurse to keep Albert's secret. Albert was also reassured that all involved intended to keep his secret. However, this was the beginning of the end for Cashier's ability to hold onto his secret.

Once he recovered significantly to work, Albert, again, started working odd jobs for extra income. He found some steady work for State Senator Ira M. Lish. Tragically, one day when Cashier was working for the senator, Lish backed out his car unaware that Albert was behind it. The senator backed over Cashier's leg, snapping it at the hip. Lish sent for Dr. C. F. Ross, who needed to set the break. When the doctor removed Albert's trousers, he realized Albert's secret. The men all looked at each other. Albert, panic-stricken, asked the other men in the room to please keep it a secret. The men agreed to keep it from the public, but there was still one problem. Albert was now disabled. Someone would need to come in and administer to his needs. This person would need to know as well, and agree to keep the secret.

Within a short time, it became apparent that Albert D. J. Cashier would be permanently crippled and unable to care for himself. Lish and Dr. Ross met to decide what to do about Albert. They came to the decision that what would be best for Cashier was admission to the Soldiers' and Sailors' Home in Quincy, Illinois. He became a resident on May 5, 1911.

Leroy S. Scott, an employee of the Soldiers' and Sailor's Home, was placed in charge of Albert's care by the superintendent of the home, Col. J. O. Anderson. The more Scott learned about Cashier the more he became interested in his life. Scott's opportunity to document Cashier's life came when Albert needed another increase in his pension. Scott explained that if he wanted the increase, he needed to cooperate and tell the truth about who he was and his background. By the time Scott took an interest in Cashier, the veteran's mental condition varied from day to day. Albert had what Scott called "lucid intervals."

Scott started to interview Cashier. Originally, Cashier listed his place of birth as Balbriggan, Ireland, between 1843 and 1844. His birth was sometimes recorded as August 6, and in other sources, December 25. Scott assumed that Cashier lived for a time near the coast of Ireland because Albert spoke of gathering seashells as a small child. Eventually, with poking and prodding, Albert became a little more forthcoming about his life. He admitted his birthplace was Clogher Head, Ireland. An aunt, Nan Hodgers, came to mind during the discussions. Scott wrote the parish priest who confirmed that a Patrick Hodgers lived in the parish. The priest apologized that he could not come up with more information for Scott because records only went back as far as 1857.

Scott uncovered that Albert had an Uncle Dennis Hodgers, who was a sheep dealer. Cashier told Scott that Uncle Dennis emigrated to New York, where he worked in a shoe factory in New York City. The only way Dennis could secure employment for his young charge was for Dennis to dress his niece "Jennie" in boy's clothing. However, Albert contradicted himself by stating that he dressed as a boy when herding sheep for his uncle. No mention was ever made of Albert's father, leading some to believe that he was illegitimate. Albert claimed at times that he also had a twin that died about the same time Albert's mother died. When asked about the name Albert Cashier, Albert explained to Scott that a man named Cashier married his mother, so he took the name.

After spending some time in New York City, Albert explained that he became a farmer. Where in New York State he farmed is not recorded. Some historians researching his life believe that Albert told many versions of his life history to keep people distant. Eventually, Albert made his way to Illinois. Again, there is a discrepancy in Cashier's account. Joy H. Saxton remembered that "he lived near here (Belvidere) for a while and worked for a man by the name of Sawyer before he enlisted, but Sawyer is dead now." Saxton served with Cashier in the Illinois 95th Company G. Saxton believed Sawyer brought him to the enlistment office in 1861. However, Albert also contradicted this statement by recounting that a man named Avery journeyed with him to enlist. When asked why he joined as a man, Albert told another veteran:

Lots of boys enlisted under the wrong name. So did I. The country needed men, and I wanted excitement. I worked on an Illinois farm as a man the year before the war. I wasn't discovered and thought I'd try my luck on the service.

Nettie Ross remembered in 1914:

He told me while he was sick that the reason he assumed the male garb was that he and another man were in love. That both enlisted at the same time; that the lover was wounded and died. That before his death he asked Albert to promise that he would never again waer [sic] women's clothes, and he said he had not.

At the time of Albert's admission, Dr. Ross and Senator Lish apprised Colonel J. O. Anderson, superintendent, that Albert was a woman and asked that he help keep the secret. Anderson agreed. None of the official records at the home list Cashier's sex as a female. Lannon writes in her thesis that because of his illness and injury, Cashier was kept mainly in his room. His secret seemed safe until he requested another pension increase. The federal government was now going to become involved, as well as newspapers.

Albert's "secret" came out to the public when he deteriorated too much for the Soldiers' and Sailors' Home to take care of him. He continued to decline mentally, becoming quite senile. Although he was not violent, he could still become loud and create disruptions. A competency hearing convened to assess the mental competency of Cashier. Believing that he no longer could manage his financial affairs, a conservatorship was granted, placing the president of the Illinois State Bank of Quincy, Illinois, as his financial guardian. Albert D. J. Cashier was declared "insane" on March 3, 1913. A new pension request for more funds was filed on Albert's behalf to cover the expenses for his continued round-the-clock care.

On the new pension request, his "true sex" was revealed, which caught federal authorities' attention. The Pension Bureau in Washington, DC, launched an investigation to determine if the individual known as Albert Cashier was the same person who served in the 95th Illinois Infantry Company G. Once an extensive investigation was launched, it became challenging to hide Cashier's secret from the press, who had a field day with it. The federal government called many witnesses, including those fellow soldiers who were still alive from Company G. As more than one historian has written, these soldiers rallied to the defense of their comrade Albert Cashier. A lot of what we know about Cashier came by way of these depositions. He continued to collect his pension after the Pension Bureau became satisfied the person collecting the pension was who he claimed to be. But the damage was done.

Albert was moved to the Watertown State Hospital in East Moline, Illinois. He was transferred on March 28, 1914. Lannon noted in her work that for the first time the paperwork recorded that Albert was a woman. Although it was determined that he would be allowed to live his life out as a man, for unexplained reasons, this did not happen. Albert Cashier was confined to the women's ward and was forced to wear women's clothing. Some recorded that it left him broken, and he had no idea that his secret was out in public. Albert just lacked experience navigating life in a dress, and as a result, Cashier tripped and fell frequently. One fall resulted in him fracturing a hip, which led to an infection.

Albert D. J. Cashier passed away at the Watertown State Hospital on October 10, 1915, at 2:30 in the morning. There was a full military ceremony in East Moline. His body was then brought back to Saunemin for burial in the Chesebro burying ground in the Sunnyslope Cemetery. Initially, the military erected a simple headstone that read "Albert D.J. Cashier Co. G 95 Ill Inf 1843-1915." Later the citizens of Saunemin erected a larger stone that included his name, company, and the name Jennie Hodgers as well as Albert's birthplace in Ireland. Still later, Albert's house was identified and preserved. Today, it is across the street from where he would have known it to have been and designated a museum. Robert Horan, a private in Company G, summed it up best after he found out "Al" was a woman: "She made a good comrade. She was a soldier with us, doing faithfully and well."

CHAPTER TEN

Mary Galloway (Wounded at Antietam)

ACCORDING TO HISTORIANS, MORE THAN FOUR HUNDRED WOMEN JOINED the Confederate and Union armies during the Civil War. Why they enlisted and how they enlisted is as varied as the women who joined. Some needed the money by way of bounties or monthly wages. Some others felt it was their patriotic duty to help end slavery or keep the Union intact from the traitorous Southerners. A sense of adventure was often quoted by some of the women years later when they were interviewed. Some women enlisted to be closer to sisters, fathers, and sometimes to be closer to a lover or spouse, as was the case with Mary Galloway.

How did these women escape detection when joining the army in this time when it was against the law for women to be in the military? Physicals or at least comprehensive physicals were nonexistent or not typical. Before the 1870s, rarely were individuals even required to strip. Many women, such as Mary Galloway, were discovered when they were wounded and needed medical attention. Galloway never had to worry about the physical prior to joining because she joined the 3rd Wisconsin just before the Battle of Antietam. She stole a Union private's uniform and attached herself to the rear guard. No one questioned her. The founder of the Red Cross, Clara Barton, discovered Mary's secret.

Mary Galloway was from Fredericksburg, Maryland. In 1861 she was sixteen years old when she met Lt. Henry Barnard. An officer with the 3rd Wisconsin, he was quartered in the Galloway house while stationed in Fredericksburg. Whether Mary's father knew they were courting is not known, but the two sparked. When Henry shipped out, they agreed to stay in touch. When the 3rd Wisconsin returned to the Fredericksburg area, Mary reunited with Henry only to have him torn from her again with a significant military engagement on the horizon.

Antietam was fought from September 16 to 18, 1862. It is known as the bloodiest single day of fighting in US history. Over twenty-two thousand soldiers from both sides fell on the three days of battle. The battle was technically a stalemate. However, the Union's showing allowed President Lincoln to issue the Emancipation Proclamation, giving freedom to slaves in those states in rebellion against the United States.

In her private's uniform, Mary Galloway joined the Army of the Potomac, commanded by Maj. Gen. George McClellan. The Army of the Potomac assaulted Gen. Robert E. Lee's forces along Antietam Creek on September 17, 1862. The morning saw Union attack and Confederate counterattacks by Gen. 'Stonewall' Jackson's brigades through Miller's Cornfield, across the Hagerstown Turnpike and into the West Woods. Mary was with the 3rd Wisconsin on Hagerstown Turnpike when a bullet struck her in the neck and exited out her back.

Galloway fell to the ground where she would lay agonizing for over twenty-four hours. It seemed she would die not having found her Henry. When the fighting was over, soldiers combed the battlefield for wounded and Mary was found. She was brought to a hospital where she again had to wait to be seen by the surgeon for another day. According to Stephen B. Oates in his book *A Woman of Valor: Clara Barton and the Civil War*, it was F. H. Harwood, the surgeon for the 3rd Wisconsin, who realized that this private was, in fact, a woman. He left to locate Barton. Harwood explained that "he had just spoke to a wounded girl lying in an open shed hospital down the road; she was wearing a Union uniform, was shot in the neck. . . ."

Probably from lack of blood, water, and pain, he reported that she was frantic and would let no one touch her, and he requested Barton's help with the matter. Once again, according to Oates, Mary was brought on a wagon to Barton. She remembered that it was easy to mistake Mary as a boy. Her hair was cut short, and she was very slender.

After gaining the trust of Galloway, Barton probed the wound in her neck and back. It appeared to her that Mary might die from the injury.

The wound was a serious one because of the loss of blood and the genuine potential for infection. It did not help that the bullet could not be extracted from her body. When Barton called over the doctor, he decided it would be better to operate than not operate. Oates explained that the doctor did not have chloroform to put the young girl under for the operation. What they did to ease the pain is not stated, but it could have been something as simple as copious amounts of alcohol.

It was a miracle that she did not die during the operation or perish from being left unattended for such an extended period of time waiting to be seen by the surgeon. Such long waits were not uncommon because surgeons were frequently overwhelmed by the sheer volume of casualties. Much later in an April 1883 edition of the *St. Louis Magazine Illustrated*, Barton and Harwood recounted taking care of Mary Galloway. Barton also recorded some of her experiences with Mary in her papers. Operating on a girl in a soldier's uniform would have stood out in both individuals' memories, even though Galloway was not the only woman to see action during Antietam.

Barton remembered questioning how this young girl ended up in an army uniform and on a battlefield. Mary Galloway recounted the story of Henry (Oates in his book records his name as Harry). She told the nurse how she went looking for the lieutenant to be with him during the battle. Mary feared never seeing him again and had to tell him how much she loved him. If he was to die in the battle, she would be with him; maybe the two would fall together and spend all eternity together.

Once Mary could go back to Frederick, Maryland, she went back to the home where she lived. She had not found Barnard and had almost died in the attempt. However, the two would be reunited shortly. Unbeknownst to Mary, Lieutenant Barnard had been wounded in the epic battle as well. He lay in a hospital needing to be operated on for a wound in his left arm. The arm needed to be amputated because gangrene had started to affect it. If surgeons did not operate soon, he would die.

Delirious from the infection and pain from the wound, Lieutenant Barnard screamed out for someone named Mary. The lieutenant refused to let the doctor come near him to amputate unless they could have Mary by his side. It is quite possible that he simply wanted to see her one last time before he died. Soldiers knew that amputations frequently ended in death for the patient. When Clara Barton was called over to assist in getting the man under control, Barton made the connection that this was the love of Mary's life.

Recalling the event later, Barton remembered leaning over the officer to tell him that she had treated Mary and knew where she lived. If he settled down, she would fetch the young woman. When Mary arrived, according to Barton, the two were overcome with emotion. Lieutenant Barnard allowed the surgeon to remove the arm. The two had finally been reunited.

Oates wrote in his book that Barton remembered that the two were eventually married. The couple paid homage to Barton, who reunited them, by naming their daughter Clara Barton Barnard. After this, the Barnards are lost to history.

There is little or nothing known about Mary Galloway or Henry Barnard. Their names are most likely aliases. When looking through military records of those soldiers wounded from Wisconsin, the name Barnard does not appear. Equally, in the census information, Mary does not appear under Galloway or Hartwell. There is a Henry J. Barnard in the New York 108th Infantry Company B. He was age twenty-two, enlisting in Rochester, New York, on July 29, 1862, as a private. He was wounded in action on September 17, 1862, at Antietam. Barnard was finally discharged for a disability on February 11, 1863, at Harrisburg, Pennsylvania. However, it does not appear that he married a woman named Mary or had a child named Clara Barton. It is possible that over the years, the names and stories were distorted. Perhaps, Mary and Henry wanted it to stay that way so they could live out their lives.

Chapter Eleven

Florena Budwin
(Woman Prisoner at Andersonville)

Florena Budwin was born sometime around 1844 in Philadelphia, Pennsylvania. There is not much known about the early life of
Budwin prior to her enlistment in the Union army. Like more than a
few women who disguised themselves as men, she did so to be with her
husband. She enlisted at age twenty-one. The name she used to enlist is
also lost to time, and her name and that of her husband John Budwin
are absent from military records. All that is known about John Budwin
is that he became an artillery captain in the Union army. We can piece
together more about Florena because her time in the military during the
Civil War was nothing short of remarkable.

A lot of what we know about Florena comes by way of an interview
that appeared in the *Helena Independent* on June 24, 1890. Newspapers
were more sensationalist in the nineteenth century. Stories of women
disguising themselves as men sold newspapers; they were intriguing to
readers, not only because of the Victorian notions of love, for example,
a woman following her husband into battle, but also because it was so
out of the ordinary during a time of narrowly defined gender roles. The
newspaper did not interview Florena but an individual by the name of
Samuel Elliott.

Samuel Elliott enlisted as a private in the 7th Pennsylvania Reserves
Regiment. He remembered that Budwin was captured during the Battle
of the Wilderness, which was fought between May 5 and May 7, 1864,

between forces led by Lt. Gen. Ulysses S. Grant and Gen. Robert E. Lee. During this battle, over one hundred sixty thousand troops fought what became an inconclusive engagement with almost thirty thousand combined casualties. In an unfortunate occurrence, both Florena and her husband John were captured by the Confederates. Both of them were eventually sent to the Andersonville Prison, a notorious Confederate prisoner of war camp located in Georgia.

Elliott recollected that the prison was "surrounded by a high stockade built of heavy pine logs and closely guarded by numerous sentinels who stood on elevated boxes overlooking the camp." In the "centre of the camp is a stream of dirty water so warm and greasy we can scarcely drink it." In his diary, Samuel Elliott continued: "about eight feet from the stockade was a low rough built railway called 'the deadline,' to lay a hand on or pass which was death from a guard musket." Captain Budwin never made it out of Andersonville. Some accounts relate that he died during the Battle of the Wilderness rather than being captured. Still others maintain that he moved too close to the deadline and a Confederate guard quickly shot him down.

Both Florena and Samuel Elliott were at Andersonville for only a short time. In his diary about life in Andersonville Prison, Samuel Elliott wrote that after leaving Andersonville, they traveled about "two hundred and fifty-nine miles" to Florence Stockade, located in South Carolina. This was during the first two weeks of September 1864. Florena, along with other troops, was moved from Andersonville to the Florence Stockade located in Florence, South Carolina. They were relocated because the Union Army was getting closer to Andersonville and quite possibly liberating it after Atlanta fell to Sherman's Army on September 1, 1864. Accoding to a nomination form for the national register provided by the National Park Service, "Florence was chosen because it was at the intersection of three railroads and provided easy access." According to the National Park Service who administer the site, it was "modeled after the prison at Andersonville." Florence had been built in September 1864 by slaves owned by Dr. James H. Jarrott. It housed some twelve thousand prisoners existing on "cornbread, molasses, and rice—when available." The military prison was part of a plantation owned by Dr. Jarrott, "a union sympathizer." Described as six feet tall, with gray hair and blue eyes, Jarrott was a physician who it is believed did his best to help the sick soldiers in Florence Stockade.

Elliott summed up their new quarters in his diary: "while at Andersonville, I did not suppose the rebels had a worse prison in the South, but I have now found out that they have. This den is ten times worse than that at Andersonville." Elliott penned this when prisoner deaths peaked at twenty to thirty soldiers a day. While in prison, Elliott told the newspaper that "I knew the female prisoner at Andersonville, having seen her frequently pass our detachment on her way to the swamp for water. . . ." He remembered her as "above medium height, sunburnt, with long, unkempt hair."

He believed she left Andersonville between September 6 and September 12, 1864, for Florence. When Elliott arrived on September 14, he wrote on the 15th that there was nothing to eat and that he could hardly walk he was so weak from hunger. Meanwhile, Florena's secret had been discovered. It was being discussed all about camp. Once the men knew about it, they, for the most part, watched over Florena. Elliott reminisced that while at Andersonville and Florence, Florena had two men who watched out for her and were her self-designated protectors.

Her true sex was discovered because, with the deplorable conditions and mass of individual sickness that moved through the camp quickly, she developed an illness but did recover from it. During that illness, she was forced to go to the prison hospital where Dr. Josephus Hall examined her and discovered she was a woman.

Dr. Hall, after living in St. Louis, Missouri, moved to Salisbury, North Carolina, in 1859. When the Civil War started, he was made chief surgeon of Salisbury Prison. He was astonished that she had not been poorly treated by the soldiers but knew he needed to get her out of the main population for her safety. The camp physician immediately gave the best care that circumstances would allow.

When local women outside the camp found out a Union woman was being held in the prisoner of war camp, they gathered up supplies to send to Florena. It helped her have an easier time in the prison camp. Budwin was told that the camp was no place for a woman. She was given the option of parole to the North, but Florena flat out refused the opportunity. Instead, she remained at Florence Stockade, working as a nurse to alleviate the suffering the best she could of the Union soldiers held there. Due to the hardships of the prisoner of war camp, poor sanitation, sickness running rampant in the camp, and insufficient nutrition, Florena, once again, fell sick. This time it turned into pneumonia.

She was sent to the camp hospital to recover, but the illness was too severe. She died January 25, 1865, while Sherman's troops were advancing. Prisoners were sent to North Carolina to be paroled through Union lines, and by February 1865, the prison camp was abandoned. Florena Budwin was buried on plantation land set aside for the Union dead of the Florence Stockade. This land was eventually turned into a national cemetery.

Today Florena Budwin's grave is still visited by curious individuals. The authors of *They Fought Like Demons* write that Budwin is "a mystery that will probably never be solved." Once the cemetery became a national cemetery, she became, what is believed, one, if not the first, female soldier to be interred in a national cemetery, occupying Section D, Site 2480. Where her husband, Captain John Budwin, is interred remains a mystery to this day.

CHAPTER TWELVE

Cathay Williams (William Cathay)

IT IS UNKNOWN IF CATHAY WILLIAMS SERVED DURING THE CIVIL WAR as a woman masquerading as a man; at least historians can't prove that she did. Some people researching her life believe that Finis Cathay of the 32nd Missouri Infantry could be her. Unless a definitive document surfaces, we will never know for sure. What is definite is she was influenced by the events surrounding the American Civil War. Cathay Williams, after the Civil War, joined the newly created Buffalo Soldiers in 1866, the only known woman to join that group. Although disabled from her time with the US Army, she would be denied a pension from the US government.

Williams was born into slavery in September 1844 in Independence, Missouri. According to historian Henry Louis Gates Jr. in his book *African-American Lives*, she eventually became a house slave on William Johnson's plantation in Independence, Missouri. When she was still a young girl, the Johnsons moved to a new home just outside of Jefferson City, Missouri.

In her interview in the *St Louis Daily Times* on January 2, 1876, she did not mention anything about her early life on the plantation. She did mention that her father was a free African American. However, her mother was a slave. This meant that Cathay Williams would be considered a slave as well. William Johnson died just before the start of the Civil War. His death placed Williams's life again in limbo. She did not know if she would be sold or willed to another member of the family.

When the Civil War began in 1861, some states were torn between their loyalty to the United States and loyalty to the South. Some of these states were slave states known as border states. President Lincoln saw it as crucial to keep these states in the Union. Missouri, where Williams was enslaved, was a border state between the Union and the Confederate States. Many of these states were strategically placed, and Missouri was no exception. These border states included Delaware, Kentucky, Maryland, and later West Virginia, when it seceded from Virginia. Early on, the Union army, in 1861, occupied Jefferson City. The Union army occupied Missouri by 1862.

Missouri remained divided but loyal to the Union. It was a slave state. This did not prevent African-American slaves like Williams from fleeing their masters for the protection of Union lines. Once behind Union lines, if they were not returned to their masters, they were seen as contraband. Confiscating slaves or freeing slaves could drive border states to the Confederacy. Instead, it was viewed that if the slave's masters were loyal to the Confederacy, then the slaves, like other property, were considered spoils of war. Williams recounted in 1876 when "United States soldiers came to Jefferson City they took me and other colored folks with them to Little Rock." Slaves captured by Union soldiers were pressed into service. They served as cooks, nurses, laundresses, and manual labor. Some freedmen were allowed to join the army.

Once in Little Rock, Arkansas, along with other former slaves, she was under the supervision of Col. William P. Benton. In 1862, Benton was promoted to a brigadier general. Benton told her that she would be cooking meals. "He wanted me to cook for the officers, but I had always been a house girl and did not know how to cook. I learned to cook after going to Little Rock and was with the army at the Battle of Pea Ridge." Pea Ridge, also known as the Battle of Elkhorn Tavern, took place on March 7-8, 1862, in Arkansas. It is frequently described as the battle that allowed the Union to hold on to Missouri throughout the war.

Did Cathay Williams have another alias when she left the Johnson Plantation? According to military records for the 32nd Regiment of Missouri Infantry, a Finis E. Cathay did serve as a private in the 32nd Regiment of Missouri Company H. However, there is no compelling information to confirm definitively that this was Cathay Williams. She made no mention of prior military service. The consensus among historians that the similarities with names is just a coincidence, that Williams served in a non-combat role. She can be traced in that capacity even though information is scarce. The primary documents that historians have are an interview in 1876 and her pension application in the 1890s in which she signed both her real name and her alias.

Cathay Williams continued to accompany the Union soldiers through Arkansas as well as Louisiana. She spoke of witnessing the destruction by the invading Union troops of large stores of cotton. Williams claimed she also saw the burning of Confederate gunboats that were captured on the Red River during the Red River Campaign, which lasted from March 10 to May 22, 1864, in Louisiana. She continued to follow the troops as a cook when the army went to New Orleans, "then by way of the Gulf to Savannah, Georgia, then to Macon and other places in the South."

Eventually, she ended up being sent to "Washington City," or Washington, DC, where she began cooking for General of the Army Philip Sheridan and his officers during the Shenandoah Campaign in 1864. In addition to cooking, Williams also washed the officers' clothing. After her time accompanying Sheridan on the Shenandoah Campaign, she made her way to somewhere in Iowa and after Iowa to the Jefferson Barracks located in Missouri. Cathay remained at the Jefferson Barracks for an extended period of time. She continued serving with the army until the end of the war, choosing to stay in Missouri to cook to make money.

Sometime in 1866, she decided that joining the US Army might be the way for her since Missouri did not have much opportunity. One can speculate that it was for many of the same reasons that other freedmen and women left the South to head west. There was simply more opportunity out west for African Americans. The freed slaves could purchase cheap land and start a better life, for much of the South was in ruins because of the war. She also knew military life from spending a year following the Union army during the Civil War. Williams indicated that it might have even been to be near family.

On November 16, 1866, Cathay Williams decided to join the Buffalo Soldiers. In her interview in 1876, she claimed the primary reason she joined was that "I wanted to make my own living and not be dependent on relations or friends." Years later, she explained that the only people who knew she was a woman were a cousin and a friend who belonged to the regiment, and they "never blowed on her" or in other words, betrayed her confidence.

How was a woman able to join the Buffalo Soldiers when it was illegal at the time for women to join the armed forces? The simple answer is because there were still no uniform, comprehensive physicals in the army. Often, doctors did not even require the enlistees to strip, which would have exposed that a person in front of them was a woman. Generally, without the physical, "men" were found to be women when they were sent to the hospital or by accident. She did not know it at the time, but she was the first and only known woman ever to join the elite Buffalo Soldiers. Described as 5'9" in height, there is no doubt that Pvt. William Cathay was one of the tallest soldiers in her regiment. Private Cathay signed on to the 38th US Infantry Company A for three years. Her commanding officer for Company A was Capt. Charles E. Clark.

The Buffalo Soldiers were an all African-American cavalry and infantry formed by Congress on July 28, 1866. Due to the racism of the time, they were not allowed to have anything but a white officer. Their primary mission was to be out west fighting Native Americans. They were also paving the way for the Transcontinental Railroad. Buffalo Soldiers escorted wagon trains, and built forts as well as roads. Buffalo Soldiers were also charged with the mission to protect settlers living in the West. Competing legends suggest that they were given the name Buffalo Soldiers by Native Americans either because the Native Americans believed the soldiers' hair looked like that of the buffalo, or because they considered them to be as brave as buffalo.

After joining the 38th, Private Cathay spent his time training at the St. Louis barracks. While there, he contracted smallpox. He was placed in the regimental hospital to recover. In April 1867, Cathay marched from St. Louis to New Mexico Territory. As noted in his pension application years later, he believed that he had not sufficiently recovered from smallpox before being discharged from the hospital and sent west. His health took a turn for the worse when "crossing the Rio Grande River in New

Mexico," he had to swim in the river. In addition, because of exposure and hardship, Cathay's health took a noticeable change. William spent time disabled by illness when the company stopped at Fort Riley in Kansas. Company A eventually arrived at Fort Cummings in New Mexico Territory.

Although William Cathay was sent west to keep settlers safe from Native Americans, he did not participate in any known battles. When not ill, he went out on patrols and participated in daily military life. His most commonly listed illness was now rheumatism. According to his pension application, by May 1867, William "has been feeble both physically and mentally and much of the time quite unfit for duty." He also began to suffer from neuralgia. Private Cathay was again admitted to the hospital in July 1868 when Company A arrived at Fort Baynard. Finally, spending more time sick than on duty, Cathay was given an honorable discharge from the US Army on October 14, 1868. He was given a surgeon's certificate for dismissal due to a disability. It is essential to point out that the certificate does not mention he was a woman. In her 1876 newspaper reminiscence, Cathay told the newspaper reporter that she became tired of military life and actually informed the surgeon of her true identity. Once William Cathay left the army, he became Cathay Williams again.

After her discharge, she continued to earn a living as a cook and laundress. In 1869 and 1870, she was a cook for a colonel at Fort Union, New Mexico. She then moved to Pueblo, Colorado, living there for two years as a laundress and then to Los Animas, Colorado, for a year again as a laundress. When she was in Pueblo, Cathay married a man that she does not identify: "I got married while there, but my husband was no account." He robbed her of $100, a team of horses, and her wagon. Cathay noted that it was a good team of horses and that she sorely missed it. Williams went to the local sheriff and swore out a complaint. The man was found and eventually arrested.

She resided in these areas for short amounts of time until she finally settled in Trinidad, Colorado, in the late 1870s. After spending the remainder of the decade there, again according to Gates, she moved to Raton, New Mexico, where it is believed she operated a boardinghouse. By 1890, she moved back to Trinidad, where she entered a local hospital.

Most of what we know about Cathay Williams comes from an abbreviated life story she told to a St. Louis journalist traveling in Colorado in 1875, where he became interested in Cathay Williams's story. The St. Louis newspaper published the article in the winter of 1876. The other source for her life, as previously mentioned, is her pension application to the US government. Even with the ailments she suffered from, the journalist described her as, 'tall and powerfully built . . . muscular looking."

Suffering from multiple ailments and lacking funds to take care of herself, she applied for a pension from the US government for her disabilities after two years of service with the 38th. By this time, she had been hospitalized for almost two years. A government surgeon in Trinidad was sent to the hospital to examine her on behalf of the government pension bureau. The doctor described her as a "large stout woman." He claimed that there was no reason to grant her a pension because he could not find evidence of a disability. The doctor did note that she had all of her toes on both feet amputated, which forced her to walk with a crutch. This alone should have qualified her for a pension. Her claim would be rejected on February 19, 1892.

Unable to work and probably lacking any money, Cathay Williams all but disappeared from the public record. It is believed that she died sometime after 1892, but before 1900. Her place of burial is unrecorded and unknown. Fast forward to 2016, and her life started to gain the national attention that it deserved, but did not receive while she was alive. A Cathay Williams monument was finally unveiled in Fort Leavenworth, Kansas, where the Buffalo Soldier Museum is located. Williams's bronze bust has a rose garden around it. There is also a brief biography attached to the base of the bust.

CHAPTER THIRTEEN

Mary Owens Jenkins (John Evans)

ON MAY 28, 1937, THE *EVENING INDEPENDENT* OF MASSILLON, OHIO, reported, "I tell you fellows, Johnny Evans is a woman. Look at him! He's got the features of a woman. Look at his hands and his face—they ain't a whisker on it." In order to be with her lover, Mary Owens dressed as a man and enlisted in the army. She would fight until her sex was discovered. Although she had already been dead some fifty-six years, the Sons of Union Veterans finally gave recognition to Mary Owens, who fought in several battles, was wounded just as many times, and had her first husband die next to her in action. They decorated her grave and installed a new monument.

There is comparatively little known about Mary Owens's life during and after the Civil War. She was born in Wales, which is part of the United Kingdom. It is believed she was born sometime in 1843, but the exact year has been lost to time. According to a newspaper article from 1937, there is evidence that her father's name was William Owen. When still a young child, her family left Wales and moved to Danville, Pennsylvania. Shortly after arriving, her father started working in the coal mines, which is probably what he did back in Wales.

Meanwhile, Mary attended a local one-room schoolhouse not far from home. It was while a student there that she met a fellow student, William Evans (though other versions tell of her being a schoolteacher when she met Evans). Mary and William Evans fell in love; however, Mary's father, for some reason, did not give his daughter his approval of William. It is unknown if it was a perceived defect with William as a husband or that Mary was too young. The couple was determined to marry and planned on eloping at their first opportunity.

According to a 1937 article in the *Evening Independent* of Massillon, Ohio, a doctor's son lived next door to the Owens family. One evening, he came over to show off a brand new suit perhaps to impress Mary, who has been described as striking in her appearance. Mary looked over his suit, supposedly retorting to him, "I'll bet I could wear that suit." Taking her up on her assertion, the young man swapped the suit with Mary. He waited in another room, waiting to see her wearing his suit. The suitor waited and waited for an uncomfortable amount of time. It soon became apparent that Mary had absconded with the new suit, and might never be seen again. Mary Owens rendezvoused with William Evans, who lived closer to town. When she arrived, he proudly told the seventeen-year-old

Mary Owens
COURTESY OF THE *DANVILLE NEWS*

Mary that he had just enlisted in the 9th Pennsylvania Cavalry, Company K. It was 1861. Fearing he could die in battle, they agreed to quickly marry in Montour County, Pennsylvania.

The new Mrs. Mary Evans, dressed as a man, succeeded in fooling the mustering officer. She presented herself as John Evans, the brother of William. She would be in the 9th alongside her husband for about eighteen months. Private John Williams, a soldier in Company K, 9th Pennsylvania Cavalry, recalled that Company K soldiers often sat around the campfire, convinced Johnny Evans was a woman. They frequently commented on the messenger of Company K. Being a messenger was a good assignment for John Evans because he was not "in close contact with the rank and file."

Although the story seems to have been altered or embellished through the years, the 9th Cavalry was placed at the Battle of Gettysburg fought between July 1 and July 3, 1863. The 9th "fought like tigers," and Johnny Evans was no different in making sure messages moved through the lines between officers. He "raced back and forth to the headquarters through a veritable rain of musket bullets and barrages of cannon fire." When he arrived back at headquarters, at one point, he observed a number of the 9th's soldiers gathered around a soldier lying on the ground. One paper stated they were digging a shallow grave. Pushing his way through the circle of men, Johnny Evans saw the deceased man was her husband.

According to Mary Owens (Jenkins)'s surviving children from her second marriage, Johnny was so overcome with anger and revenge that he grabbed a musket, thrusting the bayonet into the ground. He then threw himself into battle to avenge William Evans's death. During one of the days of battle in Gettysburg, Johnny Evans was wounded, "a deep gash across the forehead—a gash, inflicted by a Confederate sabre." The same 1937 article reported that when Johnny Evans was taken before the surgeon, his secret was discovered. "Carrying a broken heart and a scar on his head, went back to being Mary Owens Evans." Many people would make their way back home to their family. Mary might not have been welcome there anymore after disobeying her father. She went instead to Broadtop City, Pennsylvania, where she spent some time recovering and mourning the loss of her husband. Mary was twenty years old.

Prior to her husband's death, John Evans had fought along with William in two previous battles. Each time John was wounded, like many women serving in combat roles during the Civil War, John did his best to tend to the wounds. If he were sent to the surgeon his secret could be discovered, and he would be discharged. After the battle where William died, John Evans continued to fight. In the book *They Fought Like Demons*, the authors believed it was a chest wound inflicted by a Minnie ball that revealed her secret, and she was discharged from the military.

While recovering in Broadtop City, she met William "Abie" Jenkins. Some called him Abe Lincoln because he looked like the sixteenth president of the United States. William was also from Wales and, like Mary's father, a coal miner. He was born in 1841. The two eventually married in 1867 and moved to Youngstown, Ohio, where they had four children. According to the 1870 census, the couple lived in Youngstown, and Abie was a boiler.

Abie had also served in the late war. He had joined the 9th Reserve Infantry (38th Pennsylvania Volunteers) on May 1, 1861, and mustered in as a private in Company E. Private Jenkins was discharged on May 15, 1863. It was a medical discharge, by way of a surgeon's certificate. These certificates were issued for a chronic illness or a disabling wound. Abie applied for an invalid pension on June 4, 1863. His military record is well documented. Both Mary and William Evans's military records are not.

After the war, Mary Jenkins lived a Victorian woman's life, casting her martial past behind her. She raised their children and was a housewife. There is not much known about her postwar years, though there was interest in her story as a woman who served in the Civil War as a man. However, to the public, she spoke little of that time. Eventually, the family moved to North Lawrence, Ohio, after 1880.

She died relatively young, even for the time, in Massillon, Ohio, in January 1884. For many years, her grave was marked with a "piece of broken marble slab from an abandoned grave." After her death, newspapers began publishing articles on her interesting life, such as a 1909 *Pittsburgh Post Gazette* story about local veterans who would decorate her grave.

In 1937, the Daniel Ritter Camp No. 93, Sons of Union Veterans of the Civil War, erected a monument above the grave of Mary Owens

Jenkins. It reads: "Mrs. Mary Owens Jenkins served in the Civil War 1861-1865. In Co. K Pennsylvania Volunteer Cavalry under the name John Evans."

Her husband Abie Jenkins lived almost twenty years after his wife died. He was always known as a man who enjoyed his liquor. Once his wife died, he became known as a heavier drinker because of his depression over Mary's death. Abie died on November 24, 1903, when he fell out of a railroad car "as it rounded a bend along the West Tremont Street Bridge." His time of remembrance would come on June 9, 2020, when a military grave was erected over his original grave next to Mary.

CHAPTER FOURTEEN

Elizabeth "Lizzie" Compton
(Johnny "Jack" Compton)

WHEN SHE WAS ARRESTED IN ROCHESTER, NEW YORK, ON FEBRUARY 20, 1864, sixteen-year-old Lizzie Compton claimed to have joined seven or eight Union regiments in roughly eighteen months of service.

Before arriving in Rochester, Compton recalled that the famous P. T. Barnum had heard about her story and asked her to come to meet him in New York City. When she arrived there, Barnum was away. Disgusted, Lizzie made her way west to Rochester, New York. When she came, perhaps having been tipped off, the police were looking for her. The police magistrate directed Chief of Police Mudgett to haul her before his court if he found her. Mudgett found Compton in "Worden's Saloon." He entered the saloon and charged her with breaking the law by joining the army as a woman and dressing as a man, then known as conduct unbecoming a woman, which fell under the umbrella law of disorderly conduct.

Lizzie did not try to run nor deny her motivations. Looking to save face, when confronted with the charge, she explained to the police chief that she would come peacefully. If he could find it in his heart, could he not handcuff her in front of everyone? Instead, Lizzie asked Mudgett to let her leave the saloon by herself as not to look like she was being arrested, and she would meet him at the jail. Mudgett thought for a moment and agreed to her request. They both exited the saloon at different times.

When she arrived before the magistrate, Compton was interrogated. She explained that initially, she lived near Nashville, Tennessee. If she remembered correctly, she was born around 1848. The exact date of her birth she did not know because both her parents died during her infancy. Lizzie, who also went by the names Jack or John Compton, explained her fate after her parents died, "like too many children are [left] to the tender mercies of unfeeling wretches." She was placed with a family who was charged with her care. Lizzie never mentioned the family by name. They mistreated her, forcing her to work long hours in the fields at hard manual labor. This type of work did not lend itself to dressing like a girl, so she wore a long work shirt. It was not the life she wanted. Compton made up her mind that as soon as the opportunity presented itself, she would run away. The possibility that presented itself was the start of the Civil War.

Lizzie's stories about her life are inconsistent. This may have been to throw off the individuals trying to find out more information about her. Also, she would need to change things each time she joined a regiment so recruiters would not catch on to what she was doing. She stayed in a regiment as long as her secret was not revealed. When she was arrested in June 1864 in Louisville, Kentucky, the local newspapers took an interest in her story. They labeled it "strange and romantic." Lizzie did not say she was from Tennessee. Instead, Compton stated that her home was in London, Canada, West. Even more impressive, she told the reporter that both her parents were still alive as far as she knew.

The Civil War started when Lizzie was about thirteen years old. This was her chance to flee her life of despair, working long days in the field, and hard labor. Although she stated that she was from Tennessee on numerous occasions, some think that she might have been from Canada near present-day Ontario. Some historians believe her name was probably an alias. The facts about her life are scarce, and she seemed to want to keep it that way. Lizzie saw her best escape was to join the Union army, but that would come later.

For Compton, securing employment as a young girl was very difficult. In the world of the late nineteenth century, women were discriminated against in just about every aspect of their lives. Employees, for the most part, refused to hire women. Factory jobs were frequently open to young girls and women. However, these jobs most likely lacked appeal to Compton, who wanted adventure. To better her chances of landing a suitable job, she put on boys' clothing. Once dressed as a boy, she secured employment working on various steamboats plying western rivers in the United States. This lifestyle did not appeal to her as much as she thought it might, and Lizzie Compton decided to join the army.

We don't know if Lizzie joined the Union because she saw an opportunity for adventure or believed in the cause of the North. If she needed money, an enlistment bonus and monthly pay would have been a great incentive. In an interview she stated her reason for joining was because she hated Rebels. The only thing she hated more than the Rebel soldiers were Rebel women. When she was arrested, an interrogator noted that her "dislike of woman-kind is one of her peculiarities, but detestation of rebel women is her specialty."

When she finally decided that the soldier's life was for her, she desired to enlist as a bugler. Faking a birthdate and wearing boys' attire, she successfully joined the Union army. She was listed as 5'1", 155 pounds with a "rather stout build." She had light hair and a fair complexion when she joined the 11th Kentucky Calvary.

Her first battle was the Battle of Mill Springs in Kentucky, also known as the Battle of Fishing Creek, fought on January 19, 1862. It was a fight over the border state of Kentucky and keeping it firmly in the Union. It would become a Union victory and helped to keep Kentucky in the orbit of the Union. It was intense close-quarter fighting. The Union soldiers prevailed when they rallied and drove the Confederates from the field. Jack Compton noted that he was "skeered" when the action on the Cumberland River commenced on January 19, 1862. After this battle, Compton claimed that he never was scared again during the battle. If anything, he kind of liked the thrill of the fight.

In the summer of 1862, Private Compton also related that he was captured with his company by Brig. Gen. John H. Morgan and his cavalry of Confederate guerrillas known as Morgan's Raiders. They were caught near Gallatin, Tennessee, on August 12, 1862. Eventually, Jack was paroled and rejoined the Union army. He would go on to fight more in the Western Theater in the Army of the Cumberland. Compton would be present at the battles of Fort Donelson from February 13 to February 16, 1862, followed by Shiloh on April 6 and 7, 1862. He finally left the Western Theater of the war when he was discovered to be a woman.

This occurred when there was a horse in the camp that no one else could ride or was afraid to ride. Looking to prove himself to his comrades, Compton mounted the horse without a saddle. The horse reacted by throwing Lizzie to the ground. He tried to avoid visiting the surgeon, but it became apparent that he was seriously injured. When he eventually was forced to see the camp surgeon for care, Jack's secret was discovered. He was discharged after he was allowed time to recover from his injuries. He was undeterred, and once released from camp, he simply joined another outfit. This became a pattern of Compton's. Either he was discovered by a surgeon and sent from camp, or he left when he felt fellow soldiers were beginning to suspect him of being a woman. Once again, whether discharged or deserted, Compton simply rejoined another regiment.

According to Larry G. Eggleston, in his book *Women in the Civil War: Extraordinary Stories, Spies, Nurses, Doctors, Crusades, and Others*, after her accident with the horse, "she moved to the eastern theater and joined the 79th New York Infantry Regiment." She was now in the Army of the Potomac. Private Compton would fight in the epic battle of Gettysburg on July 1–3, 1863. She was discovered again shortly after Gettysburg.

A day after Gettysburg, some chroniclers of her life have written that she was also involved in a squabble with another soldier, which resulted in her being shot in the shoulder during the battle of Green River, also known as the Battle of Tebb's Bend. Tebb's Bend is in Kentucky, some six hundred miles from Gettysburg, so it is unlikely that she could have been in both these places. Such discrepancies are common when sorting through various re-creations of her life story. Some people who have written about her life also have her being wounded in the Battle of Antietam the previous year in 1862. After being discovered, Compton was again discharged from the Union army.

Compton would be in other monumental battles, including the Battle of Fredericksburg from December 11 to December 15, 1862. The struggle involved a total of almost two hundred thousand soldiers, with the Union forces being led by Maj. Gen. Ambrose Burnside, the commander of the Army of the Potomac. He crossed the Rappahannock River to attack both flanks of Gen. Robert E. Lee's Army of Northern Virginia, which occupied the top of what was called Marye's Heights, successfully repulsed Burnside. It was a Union loss. A Confederate shell exploded near Compton during the battle, wounding him in the side. A shell fragment forced Jack to the hospital where he would be discovered by the surgeon. A news reporter wrote about Jack Compton after it was revealed that he was, in fact, a she, "the girl is familiar with the use of a musket, understands the manual perfectly, has performed picket and other duties of camp and field, and delights in the service."

Eighteen months from the time she first joined the Union army, she was sixteen years old and being interrogated by a police magistrate in Rochester, New York. This was after being discharged from the Union army in January 1864. She made it known to the magistrate that she served as a soldier with high moral regard. After hours of interrogation, he concluded that "the girl had not lost her self-respect in the trying ordeal through which she had passed." When the magistrate reminded her that it was against the law for a woman to dress as a man, she retorted, "indeed she insisted that she would prefer any punishment— even death—rather than being compelled to act the part of a woman." Perhaps sympathizing with her, bail was waived, and she was released on good behavior.

Once able to leave, it is believed that Lizzie Compton boarded a train in Rochester. Some believe she left the United States for Canada, West, near present-day Ontario. Perhaps as some thought that was her home. A newspaper ran an article that in June 1864, she was in Louisville, where again she was arrested and charged with disorderly conduct. After this last arrest, what became of Lizzie Compton is not known. Many local and professional historians have tried over the years to substantiate her stories of serving over eighteen months in the Union army or even where she went after the war ended. Because of the contradictory nature of many of the events she cites, including where she lived, much of her life's questions are unanswered, including her final resting spot.

Chapter Fifteen

Sarah Malinda Pritchard Blalock
(Sam Blalock)

Sarah Malinda Pritchard was born on March 10, 1839, in Cald-well County, in the mountainous region of western North Carolina. In the community that she lived in, she went by the name Malinda, not Sarah. A determined woman, she wanted to be with her husband. If they were to die in the Civil War, they would die together. Malinda is believed to be the only woman from North Carolina to disguise herself as a man in order to fight alongside her husband in the Civil War. She is also believed to be the only woman from North Carolina who served on both sides of the conflict. At different times, she was a soldier in the Confederate army, Union army, a bushwhacker, scout, guide, and finally had a job enlisting recruits.

Malinda Pritchard was the daughter of Alfred and Elizabeth Pritchard. When Malinda was born, she entered an already large family. She would be the sixth of nine children. Unfortunately, there is little known about her early life in what was known as Watauga, North Carolina.

Some believe that she met her future husband, William McKesson "Keith" Blalock, in the one-room schoolhouse they attended. In his book about women in the Civil War, Eggleston writes that the two lived roughly five miles apart from each other. Their marriage on June 21, 1856, was something of a miracle because the two families were enmeshed in a feud that spanned over a century.

Sarah Malinda Blalock holding a picture of her husband, Keith

Neighbors remembered William as "6' tall with a light complexion, blue eyes, and light hair." William was born on November 21, 1836. In *A History of Watauga County, North Carolina*, John Preston Arthur wrote that his childhood friends gave William the nickname "Keith," which originated from a well-known professional fighter named Alfred Keith from the area. Alfred was considered a great fighter, and because Keith Blalock liked to fight and was good at it, the nickname stuck for the rest of his life.

Keith and Malinda were married at the Presbyterian Church in Coffey's Gap near where the couple lived on Grandfather Mountain. Coffey's Gap was named for Keith's stepfather Austin Coffey, and this is where his family settled. Keith's father had died shortly after he was born.

When the nation descended into Civil War, North Carolina left the Union on May 20, 1861, with the rest of the South. Those living in Watauga split even further into pro-Union and pro-Confederate camps. Austin Coffey was pro-Union. He had a close relationship with Keith, and it is believed that Keith became a Union man because of his influence. The Blalocks and the Coffeys were torn apart over their allegiances. Although a Union sympathizer, Keith hoped to stay out of the conflict and continue farming. However, he quickly realized not joining the Confederate army could endanger his family. His attempt to ride out the war, it became clear, would not work. He enlisted on "March 20, 1862," joining Colonel Zeb Vance's "Company F in the 26th North Carolina Regiment." He was given a bounty of $50. This according to both his pension request and *Women in the American Civil War*, edited by Lisa Tendrich Frank, which are both comprehensive sources into the lives of these individuals.

When Keith told Malinda of his intentions to join the Confederacy, she did not want to be away from him. While he was heading to the recruiter, she put on men's clothing and cut her hair to look like a young man. Legend has it that his wife caught up with him, and the same day Keith enlisted, Malinda also joined the same regiment, the 26th North Carolina Regiment, CSA. According to her Confederate Service Record, she was given a $50 sign-on bounty.

Capt. J. R. Ballew enlisted Malinda as Sam Blalock for "3 years or the war." She told Ballew that her name was Samuel or Sam for short, and that she was Keith's brother. Sam was a real person, Keith's cousin. They were both privates and shared the same tent.

Pvt. James Moore, a neighbor of the Blalocks who was already in the 26th North Carolina Regiment when the Blalocks enlisted, remembered that when the regiment was facing its first test in battle, the Battle of New Bern, he was "absent on detail at home to get recruits." Private Moore believed he recruited "about 45 men, among whom was a young man who went by the name Samuel Blalock." He did not know at this time that Sam was really Sarah Malinda Blalock, but he had a sneaky suspicion something was not right. She had cut her hair to look more like a young man. Still, Moore thought that Sam was familiar to him. Finally, he figured it out; Sam looked an awful lot like Sarah Malinda Blalock and was about the same height and weight, 5'4" and 130 pounds. When he remarked to Keith several times that Sam looked a lot like Keith's wife Malinda, the couple became alarmed.

Eventually, while in Salisbury, North Carolina, Keith and "Sam" pulled Private Moore aside, taking a risk by confiding in him their secret. During this time, women were forbidden from joining the army, let alone fighting. It was against the law, and Malinda could be jailed or fined. Women dressed as men was flat out against the law. After listening to the couple's story, Moore, for whatever reasons, gave them his assurances the secret would be kept between the three of them. It was too good a secret for the private to keep. He did tell at least one other person, his brother-in-law, Isaac N. Corpening, who was also in the same regiment.

According to Private Keith's pension affidavit, the couple planned to join the 26th North Carolina Regiment because they believed it would be stationed in Virginia close to Union lines. When given the opportunity, they both wanted to desert to the Union troops. Maybe they could start a new life in the North after the war. With Malinda beside him, he did not have to worry about how his defection would affect her. Unfortunately, their first attempt to reach Union lines failed. The 26th "was not sent to Virginia but to Kinston, North Carolina." The couple had to come up with a different plan.

In their short time in the 26th North Carolina Infantry, Malinda and Keith were involved in three skirmishes. It was in a third battle that

Malinda was shot in the shoulder, when the 26th was scouting for "partisans who were aiding the Federal scouts for General Ambrose Burnside's advancing army." The battle occurred when the 26th was wading across the Neuse River. The 26th was fired upon by Union forces forcing the Confederates to retreat across the river. During this retreat, Malinda was taken to the regimental surgeon by Keith. A few writers about Malinda's life allege that this is the first time she was discovered as a woman, when her shirt needed to be removed to dress the bullet hole. The regimental surgeon realized that Sam Blalock was a woman. He explained it was his duty to report Malinda and have her discharged.

Keith and Malinda pleaded with the doctor to keep it quiet. He agreed until she could return to active duty, which would be a short amount of time in his opinion. Once this happened, he would have to report Malinda. She would have to be discharged from the army. The stories merge about how Keith secured his discharge from the Confederate army and later that of his wife, who steadfastly wanted to be by her husband's side.

When Keith could leave camp without being seen, he took off for the woods around the camp. He looked for some poison sumac, which is abundant and was not hard to find. Keith stripped naked and started rolling all over the plant. He took bunches of it, making sure that every part of his body became covered in the oil. The next day Keith looked horrible. So horrible did he look that he was sent to the regimental hospital. A surgeon looked at his condition with a puzzled look on his face. He was sent back to his tent, but this did not help him. Keith's officer sent him back to the surgeon. By the second day, his skin was blistering badly, his eyes swelled almost shut, and he had a fever. When doctors asked Keith if he ever had this condition before, Keith "told doctors that a recurring and highly contagious disease plagued him." While examining him, they also found that he had a hernia. The doctors agreed that he needed to be discharged for this contagious disease. This did not resolve what to do for Sam because he had no excuse to leave the army—or did he? Even though the doctor would have had her discharged, she decided that she wanted to control her destiny.

James Moore, in a letter to the *Morning Post*, in 1900, stated, "that night his wife made it known to Captain Joe Ballew, her captain, that

she was not Sam Blalock, but Malinda, the wife of Keith Blalock."
When Ballew took her to Col. Zeb B. Vance's tent, she was not ready
to divulge her secret yet. Maybe she had second thoughts and feared
she could be thrown in jail. She wanted to be with Keith. Instead, she
asked the colonel for a leave. Colonel Vance looked at the private for a
minute. He then became indignant that this soldier dared to ask for a
leave when she was so new to the regiment. Other soldiers deserved a
furlough more and had been in the ranks longer. He flat out told her no.
He forced Sam's hand.

Pvt. Sam Blalock, matter of fact, told Vance that he was Malinda
Blalock. She also explained that she was also the wife of Keith Blalock,
who was recently discharged for a contagious disease. One can only
imagine the look on the colonel's face after Sam's statement. No doubt
there was silence. The colonel then asked Private Blalock to prove he was
a woman. Malinda was all too willing to oblige, but Vance stopped the
soldier quickly. Colonel Vance granted her an immediate discharge, and
Keith and Malinda were both discharged on April 20, 1862.

Many years later, the real Sam Blalock, Keith's cousin, confirmed
that Keith's "wife also enlisted in the Confederate Army dressed in men's
clothes and she assumed my name." He continued that after Keith was
discharged, "by reason of some bodily infirmity, his wife afterward made
her sex known, and was discharged." In her service record, it is noted
that she was forced to give back the $50 bounty. The company history
recorded that "Sam Blalock's disguise was never penetrated, which con-
tradicts the incident with the regimental surgeon." Fellow soldiers who
remembered Sam stated that "she was drilled and did the duties of a soldier as any other member of the company, and was very adept at learning
the manual and drill." Their anger with the couple would later be directed
at the new role they would play in the Civil War.

Keith and Malinda made their way back to Grandfather Mountain.
According to John Preston Arthur, the local remedy for poison sumac
was strong brine, which needed to be applied numerous times per day to
the blisters. His "affliction" cleared up pretty quickly. When his neighbors
loyal to the Confederacy saw that Keith was okay and cured, they started
questioning his motives for claiming he was sick. He did pretend that he

had a flare up of a chronic illness when in fact he created it with poison ivy. When they badgered him to reenlist, he quickly showed them his medical discharge. His neighbors, loyal to the Confederacy, contacted the authorities to investigate the matter. When questioned by neighbors and a recruiter, Keith also showed them his discharge papers. Numerous times, not believing the discharge's validity, soldiers showed up to arrest Keith Blalock at his cabin. According to W. T. Jordan Jr., in an article about the couple, "they lived for a time in a hut on Grandfather Mountain, where several other deserters joined them."

The couple were continually harassed by soldiers looking for men to take into the army. To avoid the near-constant harassment, Keith and Malinda fled deeper into Grandfather Mountain with the other deserters and Union sympathizers. Arthur believes that the couple at one point, lived in a rail pen, then a cave, and noted that on "one occasion Keith was so hotly pursued that he was shot in the left arm, and had to take refuge with some hogs which had 'bedded up' under the rocks." Soldiers did eventually catch and arrest Keith. He was confined in a guardhouse in Watauga, where he was held for eight days. On the ninth day, Keith was taken out of the guardhouse to travel to a Confederate prison named Castle Thunder. Keith would finally make it to Virginia, but not the way he wanted to arrive. He had no intention to wear what he referred to as "the Ball and Chain." While being transferred, he managed to make his escape, returning briefly to fetch his wife.

While retrieving his wife, he again was captured. This time realizing just how unsafe Grandfather Mountain had become for them, the couple managed to make it past the guards by taking back trails through the mountains to Knoxville, Tennessee. Knoxville, at this time in the war, was in possession of the Union army. Keith and Sam enlisted with the 10th Michigan Cavalry on June 1, 1864. Keith was given a $100 bounty for enlisting. The couple's new job would be to work as recruiters where they used to reside. Some neighbors testified that they had seen Keith in "full uniform of a federal soldier and with authority to enlist recruits for the U.S. Service." Malinda also donned a Union uniform.

Keith and Malinda Blalock crisscrossed throughout the Blue Ridge and the Great Smoky Mountains of western North Carolina and eastern

Tennessee. They both knew the mountains well. In addition to serving as recruiters, they served as scouts for the Union army and guided Confederate deserters and pro-Unionists to enlist in the Union army. Finally, they assisted Union soldiers who had escaped from Confederate prisons back north again to Union lines. When neighbors heard about the new role of the Blalocks, it created a lot of hatred from those who saw what they were doing as traitorous. Retribution, as we will see, was sometimes taken out on family members left behind.

When they were not serving the above functions, the Blalocks were employed to sow fear and destruction as Union partisans. Locals just used the term bushwhackers. They mainly operated in Caldwell and Mitchell Counties. Bushwhackers were considered irregular troops, soldiers who used guerrilla tactics during the war. Sometimes, they attacked settlements, attacked Union supply lines, and used ambushes quite effectively. According to the *North Carolina Encyclopedia*'s article by W. T. Jordan Jr., since they knew the North Carolina mountains so well, the couple worked with "the partisan unit of George W. Kirk in 1864."

Colonel Kirk was in command of the 2nd and 3rd North Carolina Mounted Infantry, US Army, seen by locals as primarily made up of deserters and bushwhackers. Kirk himself was a pro-Union Southerner. The regiments he raised came mainly from other pro-Unionist Southerners in North Carolina. He was seen as a traitor to the South's cause, and his raids were destructive, especially the attack on Camp Vance. He was particularly hated because he foraged with his troops off of Confederate loyalists. Frequently they took most of the supplies they needed from homeowners, and what they could not carry or needed was destroyed. Many neighbors wanted to see Malinda, Kirk, and Keith dead. Some felt that Keith returned with his wife to Grandfather Mountain, while a partisan, to settle some old scores with their rivals. Keith believed that the person who shot him in the arm, when he had to seek shelter with pigs to avoid being killed, was Robert Green.

One day while the Blalocks and some other Union sympathizers were on the road near where they had lived, Keith recognized Green coming up the road in his wagon. The bushwhackers chased down Green. Blalock pursued Green down the side of a mountain embankment, raising his rifle, and shooting Green down. Keith left Green for dead, placing him back in his wagon, and directing the wagon toward Green's home. Green did not die but survived to tell the story of his attempted murder by Keith Blalock. Both sides later had conflicting accounts of what happened on the road. This would be but one of the numerous raids by the Blalocks and their band in the area where they once lived in North Carolina.

In his book on the history of Watauga County, Arthur remembered that "up to the spring of 1864 the Union element in the mountains had been rather timid, but as the tide of battle turned against the Confederacy, Union soldiers and bushwhackers infiltrating the mountains became more numerous." In the spring of 1864, the Blalocks were part of one such raid on Carroll Moore's house.

James Moore, who recruited the Blalocks, was Carroll Moore's son. He recounted that while he had been home recovering from a wound he received in Gettysburg (according to James, he was wounded at the top of Cemetery Ridge when hit by a Union shell fragment), the Blalocks and the rest of the soldiers attacked the home. However, they were repulsed when the Moores put up a tenacious fight. Their family would be targeted again in the fall of 1864 when the home was attacked. This time James was not present but back with his regiment. His father and Jesse Moore were in the house. In addition to Carroll and Jesse, James's younger brother William who was about fourteen years old, and his cousin Dan Moore's children William Patterson, age fourteen, and Jesse, age sixteen, were ready with their guns. It was again a furious skirmish.

During the skirmish, both Patterson children were seriously wounded. James Moore stated in retelling what he knew of the attack, that both were crippled for life due to their injuries. However, he was glad to report that "Jesse Moore used the ball-and-buck shot cartridge, and the shot is still in Blalock's head." During the same skirmish, Malinda was wounded agan in the shoulder. Keith had a more severe wound. He was shot in the head, which destroyed his right eye. In addition, he was also wounded in the arm, which left the arm useless for the rest of his life. Keith recounted in his pension affidavit that the shot entered near the elbow of the arm. The ball then passed down the arm and to the wrist, exiting the wrist through the five fingers disabling the left arm entirely. James believed that the reason their house was attacked twice is that his father, Carroll, had "incurred the enmity of these bushwhackers for his active exertion against them."

By the time Keith Blalock recovered from his severe wounds received in the attack on the Moores' home, the war was rapidly ending. He was seriously disabled but still was able to continue the fight. When the war did finally end, he hoped to return to his home on Grandfather Mountain with comrade in arms, Malinda, who by this time had a young child that she left with relatives while she fought alongside her husband. After the war, the couple did return to their mountain. However, some of their neighbors were not going to allow them to forget the role they played. Some believed they were little more than murderers and robbers. The retribution continued during the early days of Reconstruction.

Three months before the end of the Civil War, Keith's stepfather Austin Coffey was murdered by those who believed him to be a Union sympathizer on February 26, 1865. Still others thought it was done as retribution for the conduct of Keith Blalock, his stepson. Still others believe he was killed because the Home Guard believed that he gave his stepson food and shelter. Organized after the Confederate Conscription Act, the Home Guard's mission was to find anyone evading the draft or who harbored Union sympathies. After Austin was killed, his body was dumped in the woods. Keith became enraged. He was determined to avenge Austin's death even if it took him forty years to do it, he reportedly exclaimed.

Keith was sure it had been John B. Boyd who recognized Austin and arrested him, which led to his stepfather's death. Almost a year to the day, in 1886, J. P. Arthur recorded in his history of Watauga County, "Boyd and William T. Blair were going from a house on which they had been at work when they met Blalock and Thomas Wright in a narrow path. . . ." After a short struggle where Keith claimed Boyd struck him repeatedly with a cane, he had no choice but to level his Spencer Rifle and kill Boyd. According to Keith's half-brother David M. Coffey, Keith attended the funeral the next day. He stood and stated:

I have always come and gone in the Globe as a free man, but yesterday I was attacked and had to kill the man whose funeral you are wit-

nessing. I expect in the future to come and go here as freely as I have in the past.

Afterward, Keith returned to his cabin on Grandfather Mountain, where authorities caught up with him. They arrested Keith with the intention of placing him on trial for the murder of Boyd. Before this could be accomplished, the governor of North Carolina, a Republican, pardoned Keith. He believed that as Keith maintained Boyd's killing was a self-defense case, because Boyd attacked Keith first.

After the war, much of what we know about the Blalocks comes from Keith's pension request to the US government. Also, a valuable resource is the US Federal Census. Probably because neighbors held a considerable amount of hatred for the proclaimed Republican Keith Blalock, the couple left Grandfather Mountain. The family ended up in Lynnville, North Carolina. Their family continued to grow, with their first child born in 1863, named Columbus. Three more children would be delivered between 1863 and 1874. Keith worked as a farmer when he decided to try his hand at "merchandizing." In 1874, Keith ran for a seat in the State Senate. He was soundly defeated. By 1892, it is believed that Keith and his family had packed up for Texas, eventually coming back to North Carolina by 1901, where they lived in Mitchell County.

Malinda passed away on March 9, 1901, in her sleep. She was buried in Montezuma Cemetery in Avery County, North Carolina. Distraught at the loss of his wife, Keith moved to Hickory, North Carolina, where he lived with one of his sons. He died twelve years after Malinda when the handcar he was using on the railroad picked up too much speed. When he entered a high mountain curve, the handcar flew off the tracks. Keith Blalock plunged to his death. He was buried next to Malinda.

Some of Keith and Malinda's neighbors saw them as heroes. Still others viewed them as determined people who believed wholeheartedly in preserving the Union. Others viewed them as villains, murderers, bushwhackers, and traitors. Perhaps the worst slap in the face to his Union loyalty was his headstone. It reads: "Keith Blalock, Soldier, 26th N.C. Inf., CSA."

Chapter Sixteen

Sarah Emma Edmonds
(Franklin Thompson)

Sarah E. Edmonds can be seen as a woman ahead of her time. She resisted the traditional roles that were assigned to women in the nineteenth century. Edmonds, born in December 1841 in Canada, journeyed to the United States because of what has been described as an overbearing father. She referred to her life as "enslaved." He attempted to control every aspect of her life, including marriage, insisting on arranging a wedding for his daughter. Sarah felt that women were expected to fullfill certain roles, and it was because of these societal roles that they could not reach their fullest potential and remained second-class citizens. Nowhere was this made more evident than in marriage. She pitied her mother because she saw that her mother could not reach her fullest potential in a male-centered world. Sarah E. Edmonds blazed a trail toward more equality.

Sarah recorded that her father was a farmer and a "mixture of Scotch and Irish." Her mother was French. The change in her life took place when a peddler arrived at the farm. Sarah's mother asked the man to eat dinner with the family, and he obliged. Sarah remembered that she was thirteen years old. Just before the peddler was getting ready to leave home, he saw Sarah and called her over to him. As a thank you for the family's hospitality, he handed Sarah a book by Maturin Murray Ballou. When she took the book, she saw that it was about the life of Fanny Campbell.

Sarah Emma Edmonds
Courtesy of the Michigan Archives

Campbell was from Lynn, Massachusetts, and married her longtime love, William Lovell. When the American Revolution begins, Lovell is out at sea. A British crew kidnaps him. To save him, Fanny dresses as a man and enlists on the very boat that kidnapped her husband. When she hears that the English ship captain has decided to take the men to England to impress them into the British Navy, Fanny, who goes by the name Channing, convinces the crew to mutiny. The crew takes the ships and becomes pirates, with Fanny as their captain. Fanny decides to take the boat to the West Indies where she becomes an ardent patriot.

Fanny represented a woman who was in command of her destiny. She took on a male persona and a traditionally male role. Her husband, ever loyal to his wife, listened to Fanny, swearing not to tell a soul that she was a woman. When the ship docks back in Massachusetts, Lovell continued to go off to war to fight the British. Fanny remained at home, content to keep the house and children. She kept a musket because she feared the British, who occupied Boston, might knock on her door at any time. The book is instrumental in Sarah's early life because her life loosely parallels the book, which is, by the way, fiction. Sarah explained that being given the book was "one of those peculiar little incidents which seems like God's finger pointing out the way to a struggling soul."

The next day Sarah remembered that her father had instructed her and her three sisters to go to a new field and plant potatoes. Instead of planting potatoes, they read through the first novel that they had ever seen. Sarah was sure that she did not want to live a conventional woman's life. She needed to act fast because her father started to arrange for her to be married. In fact, when she decided to leave, she was engaged. Before anything could move forward, "I most unceremoniously left for parts unknown." When she left New Brunswick, Canada, it was 1859. She was seventeen years old. She took to using the name Franklin Thompson.

Sarah Edmonds ultimately ended up in Hartford, Connecticut. She secured work for a publisher who sold family bibles. As Franklin Thompson, she would need to go door to door to make the sale. When it came down to it, she could not bring herself to knock on doors. Once her stomach began to grumble from hunger, she gathered the courage to start selling. She found that she was quite good at being a salesman.

Slowly, she gained confidence. Franklin Thompson succinctly stated how well things were going:

I made money, dressed well, owned and drove a fine horses and buggy-silver-mounted harness and all the paraphernalia of a nice turnout—took my lady friends out riding occasionally and had a nice time generally.

The next year, 1860, she returned to the farm in Canada as Frank Thompson selling bibles for the American Publishing Company. This was quite a risk because she could have been imprisoned for impersonating a man, as she acknowledged. While talking to her mother about bibles, Frank Thompson was invited for dinner. While one of the daughters was making dinner, Sarah's mother spoke of her daughter that went missing a year ago. Perhaps the salesman in front of her sparked a memory of her daughter. When she was about to reveal herself to her mother, Sarah's brother came home from the field. The salesman sitting at the table asked the young man if he had any saddle horses to sell. He accompanied the man to the barn, but became suspicious when all the pets acted as if they knew the salesman standing near them. She noticed that her dad was still nowhere to be found. He had not come home yet.

Being able to take it no more, especially when her mother commented on the resemblance that Franklin Thompson bore to her runaway daughter, the bible salesman revealed himself as none other than Sarah. Her mother refused to believe it. She looked for a mole on her daughter's face, which Sarah had removed after leaving home. Once her mother was assured the scar was where the mole was once located, she broke down crying, so excited to see her daughter. When the brother returned from the barn, he told the family that he thought it was strange how the animals acted when this stranger approached them.

Her life would change again as the Civil War started. After she made her way to the "vicinity of Flint, Michigan," she watched as troops began to mobilize. Frank Thompson felt a sense of duty to join the war effort as she saw troops leaving Flint for a rendezvous at Detroit, Michigan. "That I could best serve the interests of the Union cause in male attire—could better perform the necessary duties for sick and wounded men, and with less embarrassment to them and to myself as a man then as a woman."

She was enlisted into service by Lt. Col. J. R. Smith, Wm. R. Morse, captain, and Col. Israel B. Richardson. Pvt. Franklin Thompson enlisted in Company F in the 2nd Michigan Infantry Volunteers. On May 17, 1861, she joined for "love to God and love for suffering humanity." She was mustered into service on May 25, at age twenty.

Frank Thompson enlisted as a private for three months and afterward reenlisted for three years. He wanted to "nurse the sick and care for the wounded." Once enlisted, he went to Fort Wayne, Indiana, Detroit, Michigan, and from there to Washington, DC. While in the nation's capital, he "stood guard and picket duty, and drilled with Company F." Thompson would serve in the Union army for almost two of the three years.

Initially, Private Thompson helped with taking care of soldiers. He remembered that the hardships incurred by troops marching to Washington, DC, included not only heat-related issues, but also measles. "I returned to my company and remained in the ranks during the first fight at Bull Run."

First Bull Run as the Union named it (the Confederates called it First Manassas) transpired on July 21, 1861, with troops under Union brigadier general Irvin McDowell marching from Washington, DC, to strike a blow at the Confederate army under Gen. Pierre G. T. Beauregard camped near Manassas Junction near Bull Run Creek. At first it looked as if the predictions were right, and the war would end early with a crushing defeat of the Confederate army in Virginia that would open the door to the Confederate capital in Richmond, Virginia. It looked as if the Union army would win the day when they broke through the Confederate left flank during the battle, turning them back. However, as troops from Confederate general Joseph E. Johnston began to arrive with the then little known Gen. Thomas J. Jackson, the Confederates counterattacked breaking the Union right flank. This counterattack would earn Jackson the moniker "Stonewall." McDowell's army, in turn, was routed, retreating to Washington, DC, by July 22, 1861.

Pvt. Franklin Thompson saw the horror of the conflict. It affected him deeply seeing the soldiers with various injuries and terror in their eyes. It brought a feeling of helplessness in him. Even with these horrible feelings circulating within, he spoke of the retreat to Centreville Heights, "where troops stacked arms and threw themselves on the ground, as I supposed for the night. . . ." Private Thompson felt the most helpful place to be was the Stone Church, which became a hospital for the wounded. So many wounded arrived that Thompson did not know the whole future Army of the Potomac was in full retreat. He waited for the cover of darkness to travel the two dozen miles back to Washington, DC, arriving a total of twenty-four hours after the defeated Union army arrived.

He continued to work in the hospital in the nation's capital before being transferred to the 2nd Michigan Infantry, where he became a mail carrier and still later for the brigade to which the Second Michigan Infantry belonged. When the Peninsula Campaign commenced in March 1862, the Army of the Potomac's new commander was Maj. Gen. George B. McClellan, who replaced McDowell.

This campaign—a combined naval and land assault on the peninsula formed by the York and James Rivers that lasted until July 1862—sought to accomplish what McDowell could not complete, capturing Richmond. The base of operations would be Fortress Monroe at the southern tip of the peninsula. The campaign included several battles, including the Siege of Yorktown, Battle of Williamsburg in May 1862, the Battle of Seven Pines/Fair Oaks at the end of May, and finally the Seven Days Campaign when Confederate forces banished the Union invasion force. Richmond remained safe for the time being.

Private Thompson carried the mail during the Siege of Yorktown, from "Fortress Monroe to the troops in front of Yorktown." This was a trip, he remembered, that was about thirty to thirty-five miles a day. He remarked that because of "marauders" working for the Confederates, it was a dangerous job that all too often ended in the death of the mail carrier and loss of the mail.

Thompson briefly suspended carrying the mail during the Battle of Williamsburg on May 5, 1862. The 2nd Michigan Infantry took very heavy casualties, and Thompson assisted in evacuating the wounded to

Fortress Monroe. He remembered taking Capt. William R. Morse off the field of battle. Still later, at the Battle of Fair Oaks, from May 31 to June 1, 1862, Frank Thompson helped the regimental surgeon E. J. Bonine gather the wounded and dead. Part of this process was also identifying the dead soldiers. During this time, Thompson worked under challenging conditions because he had contracted malaria. While helping evacuate soldiers, he "was sick with the chills and fever."

Running the mail was one of Private Thompson's most challenging experiences in the army. He later wrote that when the military was "in front of Richmond," floods took down bridges over the Chickahominy. Still suffering from the effects of malaria, he sometimes had to ford rivers where bridges no longer stood. Sometimes for hours and sometimes for days, his clothing was drenched. Nighttime was the worst time to wear wet clothing because he literally shivered nonstop. He almost lost his life during the Seven Days battles from June 25 to July 1, 1862.

During the Seven Days battles, supplies for the 2nd Michigan were running low. An officer asked Thompson to forage at a local farm, asking the owners if they could spare food. When he knocked on one particular house, he secured some food and supplies for the soldiers. While leaving home, a skirmish erupted, and the private was stuck in the middle. Luckily, he was not hurt, eventually returning to camp.

When the army evacuated the peninsula in August 1862, the 2nd Michigan went into camp at Harrison's Landing. Once again, Thompson became postmaster. When the 2nd Michigan was sent to reinforce General Pope in the Shenandoah Valley, Private Thompson remained behind in camp. According to his recollections, he did not rejoin Company F until the Second Battle of Bull Run or Second Manassas at the end of August 1862. Toward the end of 1862, Private Thompson became an orderly for Gen. G. M. Poe during the Battle of Fredericksburg. He served "with such skill and fearlessness to receive commendations of field and general officers." In a letter written on September 6, 1897, she recalled an accident she suffered while carrying the mail between Washington and Centreville, Virginia, near where the Second Battle of Bull Run was about to occur.

"I was trying with all my might to reach Berry's Brigade before the battle commenced, and in order to do so, I took advantage of every near cut that I possibly could, by leaping fences and ditches instead of going a long way round." This was just before the start of the Second Battle of Bull Run. While attempting to cut some time off her trip, she tried to jump a wide ditch on her mule. The mule came up short and ended up trapped in the mud. She was thrown and hurt in the fall. Finally, she was able to extricate the mule. "On crawling out of the ditch I realized that I had sustained severe injuries. I had no use of my left lower limb. I felt sure it was broken, and the intense pain in my left side, and breast, made me feel sick and faint; while the bare thought of the undelivered mail drove me almost frantic." She was able to remount the mule to deliver the mail.

When she got back to her tent, she realized that she was more seriously hurt than she first thought. Continuing in the letter, "After the battle was over and the Army had gone into camp, I found myself in a more serious condition than when the accident occurred. I had received internal injuries which caused frequent hemorrhaging from the lungs. But I dared not report the fact nor apply for medical treatment, for the very first thing would have been an examination of my lungs—which to me simply meant 'dismissal from the Service.' Consequently, I took the utmost pains to conceal the facts in the case and silently endured all the misery and distress which the unfortunate accident entailed upon me, rather than to be sent away from the army under guard like a criminal." She credits her survival to R. H. Halstead and two other soldiers who helped her recover. She maintained a report was never filed.

As previously stated, during the Peninsula Campaign, Private Thompson had been infected by a mosquito carrying malaria. He remembered while he was in Kentucky, around March 20, 1863, he became "debilitated by chills and fever." As the condition worsened, Frank Thompson became increasingly concerned that he would end up in the hospital. If this happened, there was always the chance his secret might be discovered. To avoid this possibility, Thompson asked his commanding officer for a medical leave. The commanding officer denied the leave. Pvt. Franklin Thompson's only alternative was to desert the army, which is exactly what he did. Franklin Thompson departed Lebanon, Kentucky, on April

22, 1863, arriving in Oberlin, Ohio, "where I remained four weeks in the same costume. . . ." He took a job as a mail carrier. A captain in Company F wrote about his desertion when he found out that Franklin was Sarah: "Her sex was never suspected, and her desertion was the topic of every campfire."

Private Thompson needed time to regain his health. While convalescing, he decided that he would once again become Sarah Edmonds. However, she still wanted to help with the war effort that she so strongly believed in as a soldier. She decided to volunteer as a nurse with the Christian Sanitary Commission at Harper's Ferry, which was now part of the new state of West Virginia. It was during the period when she had deserted that she wrote her autobiography about her war experiences. It would be published in 1865 with the title *Nurse and Spy in the Union Army*. Because of the book, the federal government would never give her a pension. This was okay with her at this time, as she stated she did not want a pension because she loved her independence "too well to willingly become a pensioner on the bounty of anyone—even dear old Uncle Sam."

Shortly after the Civil War ended, Sarah returned to Oberlin to study. However, she gave up her studies and went to visit her family in New Brunswick in 1866, where she met a childhood friend, Linus Seelye. Linus was a carpenter and a recent widower with young children. The two married the following year in 1867. Sarah embraced the institution that she, earlier in her life, felt enslaved her mother. Exactly when she had a change of heart is not known. The couple would have four children, of which sadly, three died in infancy. Linus and Sarah Seelye moved to the United States, living in several different locations, including Fort Scott, Kansas. Sarah continued to do work that benefited Union soldiers.

During her life, Sarah and Linus never seemed to have a large amount of money. Sarah made a considerable sum of money from the sale of her book, but she did not see a dime from the publication because she donated all the royalties associated with her book to the welfare of the soldiers who fought for the Union. Her husband, a carpenter, had trouble finding work and also was ill near the end of his life, which reduced the family's financial means considerably. Dr. Thomas Barrett of Fort Scott, Kansas, where the couple resided, believed she suffered from heart, liver, and kidney disease. She also suffered from rheumatism. It was time Sarah took action.

Being labeled a deserter always bothered Sarah, and she needed to have this blight on her military record removed to claim a pension. She found out that it would take nothing short of congressional action to remove the charge of desertion from her military record. She had an ally in her former colonel Bryon M. Cutcheon, a congressman, who knew Sarah personally. Sarah started a speaking tour, giving interviews, and getting her story out in a public relations blitz. She became something of a celebrity, so by the time Congress took up her cause, she was well known to them.

She did not stop at her desire to secure a pension. In addition to requesting her pension, she also wanted the bounty and sign-on bonus due to her. Sarah Edmonds Seelye filed her application for a pension from the US government on November 25, 1884. Before her application, she contacted members of her old regiment, the 2nd Michigan Infantry, to secure affidavits testifying to her bravery. They would also need to attest that Sarah Edmonds and Private Franklin Thompson were the same person. Although she never claimed that she was wounded or taken prisoner she stated, "but I was disabled by accidents on three different occasions while on duty. . . ." William Shakspeare, of Company K of the 2nd Michigan Infantry until June 1864, testified that "he was a strong, healthy, and robust soldier, ever willing and ready for duty." John Robertson, adjutant general, who wrote *Michigan in the War* in 1882, stated: "She succeeded in concealing her sex most admirably, serving in various campaigns and battles of the regiment as a soldier; often employed as a spy, going within the enemy's lines sometimes absent for weeks, and is said to have furnished much valuable information."

Just as Albert Cashier's fellow soldiers had done, Sarah Edmonds's comrades in arms came to her aid. As historians DeAnne Blanton and Lauren M. Cook wrote in *They Fought Like Demons*, "Gen. O. M. Poe personally wrote a letter to Congress pleading on Sarah Edmonds's behalf. He penned the letter on January 4, 1885." General Poe believed that Sarah Edmonds and Franklin Thompson were one and the same, and he asserted that he had seen her since the war at a regimental reunion.

William Shakespeare further testified in his affidavit; the former Franklin Thompson was pushed to desert because the "application for furlough was denied, the alternative was the hospital or absence without leave." He also wrote that he believed that Franklin was "brave to the last degree." Still another comrade testified, "I shall always know you as 'Frank' my soldier friend whom I learned to respect. . . ."

Her pension took a large step forward when, on July 3, 1886, Cutcheon introduced a Bill to Remove Charge of Desertion from the Record of Franklin Thompson, and it was passed. Her official discharge date was to be April 19, 1863. She would be entitled to her bounty, back pay, and her pension of $12 a month. After her pension fight, she continued to attend reunions of the Grand Army of the Republic, becoming its only female member. She was welcomed by her former comrades of the 2nd Michigan.

After living in Fort Scott, Kansas, she moved with her husband to La Porte, Texas. In 1893, she asked for a pension increase. She was not successful, and in September 1897 decided to write to R. H. Halstead, who had been a member of the 2nd Michigan eventually becoming a sergeant, writing "my entire left side from head to my foot shows symptoms of paralysis, and it maybe, that very soon, I will not need a pension."

Sarah Edmonds was correct, for she died on September 5, 1898, in LaPorte, Texas. Although known for being a woman soldier during the Civil War, her own words summed up how she wanted to be remembered: "I went with no other ambition than to nurse the sick and care for the wounded." She was buried with full military honors by the local chapter of the Grand Army of the Republic. She was given a plain military headstone in the Grand Army of the Republic section of the Washington Cemetery. All that was included was her name, and under her name, "Army Nurse." After 1910, her husband left Texas and the home he shared with his wife, his son, Fred, and his son's family on Hill Street. Eventually, he left and went to live with family in St. Johns, New Brunswick, Canada, where he was born. He died there on June 15, 1918.

CHAPTER SEVENTEEN

Loreta Janeta Velazquez (Harry T. Buford)

EVEN BEFORE I STARTED WRITING THIS BOOK, I FOUND THE STORY OF Loreta Janeta Velazquez. It had all the elements of a great novel. Some historians feel it is just that—a novel. Did Loreta embellish her exploits during the Civil War to sell books? Whether it was fact, fiction, or a combination of both, Velazquez told a compelling story of emigrating to the United States; finding love, and marrying just before the Civil War; losing her husband early on due to an accident; marrying her husband's good friend, only for him to die as well; and spending the war as a soldier, disguising herself as a man, and still later as a double agent working for the Confederacy in Washington, DC.

Velazquez wrote an autobiography in 1876. She claimed that she was descended from Dan Diego Velazquez, the first governor of Cuba, and that her family was a distinguished one in both Spain and the Americas. Although she never mentions her father's name, she writes that he was a native of Carthagena, Spain, and was educated in the finest schools in both Spain and France. When her father got older, he was appointed a diplomat in Paris as an attaché of the Spanish embassy. This is where he met Loreta's mother, the daughter of a French naval officer and an American woman. The couple at one point lived in Madrid.

In 1840, the father and his family, which included three sons and one daughter, were sent to Cuba by the Spanish government. On June 26, 1842, Loreta was born in Havana, Cuba. The following year her father inherited a large estate in Texas, which was still part of Mexico. He left Cuba with his family, settling in San Luis Potosi in 1844. They

Loreta Janeta Velaquez

were not there long before the Mexican-American War commenced. Mr. Velazquez left to join the Mexican army to defeat the Americans. He sent his five children to St. Lucia to stay with his sister's family. When the war ended, his estate in Texas was devastated. He also refused to live under the US government. Her father gathered up his family and moved back to Cuba, where her family inherited a large plantation at Puerto de Palmas.

As was customary in wealthy families like the Velazquez family, Loreta was educated by a private tutor until 1849. When she learned all she could learn from the personal tutor and had reached the appropriate age, she was sent to a regular school. Loreta was sent to New Orleans, Louisiana, to her mother's sister, who supervised her education. She referred to her as Madame R. While being educated, her father decided that his fourteen-year-old daughter should be married. The marriage would be an arranged one. Loreta did not want to be married to the person her father picked out for her. In her autobiography, she refers to the man as Raphael R. She, in fact, was engaged to this man about whom she stated, "I did not feel a particle of affection for him. . . ." She had already met someone else, a US Army officer named William Rouch.

Rouch and Velazquez fell in love, and she started to flirt with Rouch in front of her fiancé openly. They would exchange letters and meet frequently. She wrote that she understood love for the first time and detested her beau even more than before. Continuing to see the flirtation before him, Raphael demanded that Loreta's aunt put a stop to this "affair" happening right before his eyes. The aunt told her niece that she would be sent back to Cuba, where she would never see this man again if it did not cease.

Loreta openly accepted her aunt's decree. Instead, she set up a clandestine meeting with the American officer. When he told her that he was due to be deployed any day, she became nervous about never seeing him again. He told her it would probably be one of the frontier posts. The couple decided the best course of action would be eloping. However, the couple believed they should try approaching her father and mother before they went through with it.

When she told her father about William Rouch, he became enraged. Her father had been vehemently anti-American since the Mexican-

American War. He refused to give his approval to his daughter, especially for an American soldier. Disobeying her father, she decided to elope with Rouch. They were married on April 5, 1856. She returned to her aunt's home as if nothing was wrong. Loreta finally sent Raphael away, and when her aunt threatened her, she showed her aunt the wedding certificate. When her parents found out in Cuba, she was promptly disinherited.

Between 1856 and 1860, the couple had three children, all of whom died in infancy. When it became apparent that the Civil War was imminent in the United States, Loreta convinced her husband to join the Confederacy. He bowed to her wishes and gave up his officer's commission for that of a Confederate officer. When he was mustered, Loreta became distraught at the possibility of him being off without her. Loreta proposed to her husband that she pose as a man and join the army with him. His response was for her to stay home where a woman belonged. In an effort to convince her not to join the military, while in Memphis, he allowed her to dress as a man, and they went out for a drink. This was to show her what men were like and how unsafe it would be for her in the ranks. On April 8, 1860, her husband left for Richmond, Virginia. His wife was undeterred.

Loreta found a tailor to make her a Confederate uniform. Seeing that it did not fit well, she had a local tailor continue to work with her outfit when she arrived back home. Eventually, she ended up in Arkansas, where she writes that she raised "235 recruits in 4 days." She intended to ship the men to her husband, who was now in camp at Pensacola, Florida. He, she felt, would be so happy to see her. Before leaving, she cut her hair, and attached a goatee and mustache to her face. Loreta's new name became Lt. Harry T. Buford. The soldiers she raised became known as the Arkansas Greys. When she arrived, she told her husband who she was and hoped he would approve. He did not agree and reprimanded her for her behavior. He ordered her to go home. It would be the last time she would see him alive.

She left the camp in Florida for New Orleans. When she got there, a telegram was waiting for her. While William was "drilling his men, my husband undertook to explain the use of the carbine to one of the sergeants, and the weapon exploded in his hands, killing him almost instantly," She lamented that she was "now alone in the world." She left her command in charge of Lieutenant De Caulp, and went to look for areas that would see combat. She wanted "to take an active part in the war, if only for the purpose of revenging my husband's death." Her first test in combat would come at First Bull Run/First Manassas on July 21, 1861.

When Lieutenant Buford arrived in Virginia, he went toward the Confederate Headquarters where it looked to him the action might be. He went around, asking for a command at one point, even trying to buy one. He was repeatedly told there was none to be had. According to the memoir, Brig. Gen. Milledge Luke Bonham took Buford under his command.

During First Bull Run Buford was at Blackburn's Ford. He writes that on July 18, "the enemy made a sharp attack." The Union army was repulsed during their initial attack on the Confederates, but as the attack grew more determined, the Union repulsed the Confederate army. An hour later, she remembered the Confederate army was able to turn back the attack on Blackburn's Ford, which started a Union retreat. It was the beginning of the larger battle of Bull Run. Eager for more action, she also had been placed in temporary command of a company when the senior officer had been killed. As the troops began to mass on July 21, 1861, she claimed to have no fear, although it looked as if the Confederates would lose the battle. But later in the day, the battle turned in favor of the Confederate army and it turned into a full rout of the Union army, which retreated to Washington, DC. After the battle, Buford returned to Richmond; as a freelancer soldier, he looked for other places where his services could be useful. If Henry Buford wished for more battles in which he could prove his bravery, these would come. He would be in the Battle of Ball's Bluff on October 21, 1861, which was another victory when Confederate troops beat back the Union force.

After the Battle of Ball's Bluff, Buford became Loreta Velazquez again. As a woman, she entered the city of Washington, DC. While in Washington, she acted as a spy to gain intelligence for the Confederate government. She looked for such things as troop movements, cannon placement, and other intelligence. She later claimed that she met President Abraham Lincoln and his secretary of war. When she gathered enough, she returned over the Potomac to Richmond, Virginia. She claims that she was made a detective, and that the reason she went back to being a woman was her boredom with camp life. She would return to the army as Lt. Harry T. Buford in time for the battle of Fort Donelson, where she remained until the fort fell to Grant and his soldiers. Buford was wounded in the foot during that battle, and it was severe enough of a wound to have to visit the surgeon. She left camp to return to New Orleans for treatment of the foot wound. When she returned, she was arrested.

She entered New Orleans when the city was readying for a Union attack. Suspicion and anxiety were relatively high in the city. When she appeared in the town, Buford was still wearing his uniform, albeit in tatters from battle, hard work, and being slept in for days on end. It became apparent that she might be a woman. In her words, "I was in very low spirits, if not absolutely sick when I reached New Orleans and was not in a mood to play my part in the best manner." Buford was arrested—at the "Delachaise grounds" according to a local newspaper—for being a spy and taken before the provost marshal. "I determined that the best, if not the only plan, was to present a bold front, and to challenge my accusers to prove anything against me, reserving a revelation of my identity as a last alternative." After the provost marshal questioned her, he decided to let Buford go.

The day after Buford was acquitted of being a spy by the provost marshal, he was arrested again. This time the charge was disorderly conduct or dressing in man's clothing. Buford was brought before the mayor of New Orleans. When a Dr. Root from Charity Hospital appeared to question "her" where she was staying, she knew that he would be hard to dismiss. Buford came clean that he, in fact, was a woman dressed as a soldier. She met with the mayor and asked that she be able to leave the city and never return. He would have nothing of it. Instead, he had her fined $10 and sent her to jail for ten days. After her time was up, she fled the city to rejoin the army as Lieutenant Buford. However, before the city fell to the Union, she returned to New Orleans, according to a local paper, when the Federal fleet arrived. She was recognized and arrested but managed to be released and escape back to Richmond.

After her first husband's death, Larry Eggleston writes in *Women in the Civil War* that Lieutenant De Caulp kept in touch by mail. She had known him for a long time. After William's death, he had told his friend's widow that he had strong feelings for her. He had been in love with her back when William was courting her. He just forgot about it because she was already married to him. When William died in the accident, he picked up on his feelings for her. They would fight together in Shiloh, where Buford was wounded by a piece of shrapnel when a shell exploded and lodged in his hip.

De Caulp did not know that Loreta and Harry were one and the same. In her memoir, she wrote that she wanted to tell him and not have him find out from someone else. This time would come after the Battle of Shiloh when the two had fought side by side. De Caulp was in the Empire Hospital in Atlanta, Georgia, recovering from an illness when Buford's foot was hurt again; according to the authors of *They Fought Like Demons*, the foot injury occurred when Buford was running dispatches between Richmond and Atlanta. He decided to head to the hospital, being admitted "on July 26, 1863," to see De Caulp.

While at the hospital, De Caulp was happy to see Buford. He had come to cherish the young man's friendship. The two men started talking when, according to her memoir, De Caulp produced a picture of Velazquez. He spoke about how much he missed her and loved her. De Caulp went on to say that they were to be married after the war. Buford became nervous about revealing himself to De Caulp. If she did, there was the chance that he would reject her. Instead, in a roundabout way, she led him to his discovery. When he realized that the "man" standing in front of him was none other than his love, he was joyful. The couple decided to take the doctors into their confidence as witnesses so they could be married. The doctors agreed and found a priest who also agreed to the union. They were married.

Velazquez, in her memoirs, wrote, "our honeymoon was a very brief one. In about a week, he thought himself well enough to report for duty; and he insisted upon going, notwithstanding my entreaties for him to remain until his health was more robust." She returned to civilian life as a woman. Thomas De Caulp returned to his command, but on the way, he relapsed with the undisclosed illness. While ill, he was taken prisoner by Union forces and sent to a Union prison in Tennessee where he died. She was not able to retrieve his body for proper burial. She decided there was no use in staying out of the war, and she rejoined the Confederate cause.

Eggleston, who draws mainly from her memoirs and newspapers, which are really the only sources of information about Velazquez's life, states that the first thing she did after shedding her uniform was to pay an African-American woman "$20 for a dress, sunbonnet, shawl, and shoes." She disguised herself as a poor woman heading north. Along the way, people took pity on her giving her better and better clothing as a gift. She wrote that at one point she was dressed so well that she secured lodgings in the Brown Hotel in Washington, DC. She was now a secret agent employed by the Confederate government.

During her time as a secret agent, historians Blanton and Cook write that she was arrested as a spy at least three times. One time she was arrested "for being a transvestite and suspicion of being a spy." She would be sent to Castle Thunder Prison when she was released when it was found out that she was, in fact, working for the Confederate States of America.

When she arrived in DC, she continued as a master of espionage for the Confederates reporting back to Confederate officials on troop movements, defenses, and other military intelligence. Eggleston believes that Loreta found out that the Pinkerton Federal Detective Corp. was hiring a detective. She applied using the alias Alice Williams, and earning $2 a day as a "special agent." She successfully joined their ranks, making her now a double agent. Her commanding officer at the Pinkertons told her to go to Johnson's Island Prison in Sandusky Bay, located in Ohio. There was an insurrection brewing in the prison. The detectives wanted information on the people planning the insurrection so they could crush it before it got started. Loreta, using an alias, came through Canada.

Loreta met with Confederate sympathizers in Canada and worked with operatives there in order to help the Confederate cause. She then visited the prison and helped those individuals planning the insurrection. It would ultimately fail because a prisoner turned the men in who were planning it into the authorities. This was in mid-September 1864. What is also of note is that her boss, Lafayette C. Baker, who was the chief detective of the Pinkertons in Washington, DC, felt something was off about his latest detective. He placed another detective to find out more information about her to make sure she was who she said she was when taking the job. She left the job with the Pinkertons in 1864 when she felt the job was becoming too dangerous and she could be found out. Loreta was still determined to help the Confederates. She traveled to Havana, Cuba, to secure supplies for the Confederacy. Perhaps the most intriguing bit of information uncovered by Blanton and Cook in their book *They Fought Like Demons* was "that in the winter of 1865, while in New York City, she plotted with other Confederate agents to assassinate President Lincoln." Another plot separate from that involving John Wilkes Booth was uncovered by investigators. The plot involved a "'Miss Alice Williams, who was commissioned in the rebel army as a lieutenant under the name of Buford. . . .'"

After the war ended, she married for the third time, wedding a former Confederate officer named Major Wasson. In her memoir, she described him having "long, wavy flaxen hair, which he wore brushed off his forehead, blue eyes, and fair complexion." She still did not give up her dream of the Confederate cause. She started working with the Southern State for the Venezuelan Emigration Company. They moved to Caracas, Venezuela, for the purpose of settling former Confederate soldiers. While getting ready to return to the United States, her husband contracted an illness and died. She returned to the United States, according to a local paper, by January 1867. According to her memoirs, she got married again in 1868, when she was living out west in Nevada, to a miner named Edward Hardy Bonner. She went out for many of the same reasons many other people left the South: for better economic opportunity that was not available in the war-torn South. Loreta would give birth to a son, and the family of three moved to California. It was while in California that she wrote her memoirs about her time in the Civil War. It was published in 1876, with the title *The Woman in Battle: A Narrative of the Exploits, Adventures, and Travels of Madame Loreta Janeta Valezquez, Otherwise Known as Lieutenant Harry T. Buford, Confederate States Army.*

Not everyone embraced her version of the facts. In two surviving letters from October and November 1876, she addressed one letter to the Rev. W. Jones, because she felt insulted after reading his review of her book in the *Southern Historical Society Papers*. She took great pains to point out that the version of events is her version as she saw them. It was not meant to be a historical account of the war.

She also wrote a letter to J. William Jones, D.D., who also questioned the validity of her statements. Perhaps the most famous person to challenge her version of events was Gen. Jubal Early, a former Confederate officer. Blanton and Cook write that Early read the book in 1878 "and concluded that it was false." They continue that "Early was correct in noting chronological inconsistencies" in her book.

Since the book was published, many historians have pointed out that the book had significant problems and was most likely embellished. In *They Fought Like Demons*, the authors point out that her second husband, Thomas De Caulp, did not die. He, in fact survived the war. He was part of the 3rd Arkansas Cavalry and was reported as a deserter. He later joined the Union army under an alias and married another woman.

Finally, in 2016 William C. Davis published the book *Inventing Loreta Velasquez: Confederate Soldier Impersonator, Media Celebrity, and Con Artist*; Davis maintains that most if not all of what Velazquez states is not truthful. He writes in an article from June 2017 that Velazquez reveals herself to be a prototype of the modern "'media celebrity.' A master at manipulating the press to achieve publicity. Her real name at birth remains unknown." Using newspapers to track her down, Davis came to believe she might have been a teenage prostitute in New Orleans in 1860, using the name Ann Williams. Like Jubal Early, he sees many inconsistencies in her book and goes as far as to assert that her facts change throughout her life. Davis also claims that she died much later than 1891. He believes she died in January 1923 in St. Elizabeth's home for the insane in Washington, DC. The location of her final resting place remains a mystery.

Some still maintain that her story contains truth, and it is a fantastic read for others. There is no doubt that the story of her life will continue to generate controversy for another 140 years.

CHAPTER EIGHTEEN

Unfinished Lives, Part II

SARAH EMMA EDMONDS WROTE IN HER AUTOBIOGRAPHY:

In passing among the wounded after they had been carried from the field, my attention was attracted by the pale, sweet face of a youthful soldier who was severely wounded in the neck . . . The soldier turned a pair of beautiful, clear, intelligent eyes upon me for a moment in an earnest gaze, and then as if satisfied with the scrutiny, said finally, "Yes, yes; there is something to be done, and that quickly for I am dying. I have performed the duties of a soldier faithfully, and am willing to die for the cause of truth and freedom. . . . I wish you to bury me with your own hands, that none may know after my death that I am other than my appearance indicates. . . ."

The soldier that Sarah Edmonds found after the Battle of Antietam had donned a man's disguise to serve in the war, just like Edmonds. The unknown woman died, and following the dying woman's last wish, Edmonds buried her under a mulberry tree. "I carried her remains to that lovely spot and gave her a soldier's burial."

Many of the stories we have about women who served as men during the American Civil War are because of the memoirs, interviews, or diaries they left behind. There was a fascination with women dressed as men who fought in the Civil War. This being said, it was still against the law for a woman to dress as a man, let alone fight in battle, so many women serving in the Civil War had an incentive to keep their secret quiet. Other women did not identify with the gender they were born into and wished to live their entire lives as men.

This might be the case for the above soldier who was found by Edmonds, who herself at one point dressed as a man using the alias of Frank Thompson. By the time Sarah had found the dying Union soldier, she had decided to shed her alias and become a nurse.

Women fought and died in just about every major battle of the Civil War. According to several historians, including DeAnne Blanton, during Pickett's Charge, a pivotal fight during the Battle of Gettysburg, two women fighting for the Confederacy died. Their names are still not known for sure. One soldier was killed instantly during the charge, and the other was seriously wounded and lay dying for hours near the Emmitsburg Road. After the Battle of Gettysburg was over, a Union burial detail found both women. A New Jersey private ordered to do picket duty by the Emmitsburg Road recorded that it was the worst night of his life listening to a woman who had been wounded screaming for help. He said, "Her cries were horrible; the most horrible ever heard."

Pickett's Charge, where these women were cut down, was ordered by Gen. Robert E. Lee against Maj. Gen. George G. Meade's position. It occurred on July 3, 1863, the last day of the Battle of Gettysburg. The charge was named after the major general who led it, George Pickett. It was hoped the Confederates would be able to dislodge the Union from Cemetery Hill, but they had overestimated how much the artillery bombardment on July 2, 1863 had softened up the Union defenders. When the Confederates moved on the Union troops, they were mowed down in a decisive victory for the North.

Some women did not see battle in the Civil War, but still ended up in Confederate prisons. During the summer of 1863, Capt. Harry Hunt Jr., of Buffalo, New York, owned a coasting vessel. A coasting vessel is quite literally how it sounds, a ship (usually a schooner) that primarily traded along the coast. In this case, Captain Hunt's coasting vessel traded up and down the United States' East Coast.

Harry Hunt and Janie Scadden, the latter from Chicago, Illinois, were wed in 1863. Captain Hunt took all the wedding guests aboard his coasting vessel for a ride out to sea. The ship was docked in New York City, where it is believed the wedding was held. Within a few hours of setting sail, a US revenue cutter overtook the vessel, ordering it to halt. The troops aboard the cutter boarded Hunt's ship to discuss a matter with him.

Revenue cutters helped the US Navy during the Civil War. According to the US Naval Institute, revenue cutters were the precursor to the US Coast Guard. "Cutters escorted convoys, enforced blockades, served as military command ships, participated in brown-water combat (rivers) and shore bombardments, and providing security to their homeports; they were a vital maritime force in the conflict." The captain of the cutter ordered Hunt to take his ship south to North Carolina. Once in North Carolina, he was to take on a load of corn. The problem was that all the guests, and his wife, who was pregnant, were taken with him on the dangerous mission that all would never forget.

Captain Hunt, his wife, and all their wedding guests sailed down the East Coast to North Carolina. While they were loading up the corn onto the schooner, Confederate troops captured the ship and took all aboard into custody. In a 1915 article in *Confederate Veteran Magazine*, Dr. Kerr wrote, "Finding out that the party was composed of non-combatants, all were turned loose except Captain Hunt." When faced with prison, his wife Janie refused to leave his side, even though she too was allowed to go with her wedding party. So, the newlyweds were taken to military prison. Eventually, the couple ended up in the infamous Andersonville Prison in Georgia.

When the Hunts arrived at Andersonville, also known as Camp Sumter, it was a relatively new prison. It had been constructed in the early part of 1864. The National Park Service, which interprets the site, states that it was only in operation for "fourteen months, however, during that time, 45,000 Union soldiers were imprisoned there, and nearly 13,000 died from disease, poor sanitation, malnutrition, overcrowding, or exposure." While incarcerated, Janie gave birth to a son named Harry Jr. According to the story, Janie was permitted by Confederate prison officials to dress as a man. This was to protect her, and so she could remain with her husband. Numerous attempts were made to get her to reconsider. Janie would not hear of it. She was determined to stay with her husband and would not leave the prison without him

In an article written for the magazine *Confederate Veteran*, Dr. William Jacob Warren Kerr wrote that he was transferred to the prison in July 1864 and served as the camp doctor. Kerr noted that while in his office the first night he arrived, he kept hearing the sound of an infant crying. Dr. Kerr started asking questions about why he heard a child crying in a prisoner of war camp. Kerr recollected that a Confederate prison guard explained that Captain Hunt and his wife were in a tent and had a small infant. Kerr's jaw dropped thinking of a child in the misery of Andersonville Prison. When he finally found the tent with Janie, she informed him that the child was three months old. Kerr described the conditions the couple and the infant lived in as "the most abject poverty I had ever seen."

Much of what has been written about the Hunts comes from Kerr. When he arrived, the couple had already been given a tent away from the general population of prisoners. Kerr remembered hearing, "While inside of the prison one night the Federal Prisoners cut the back of the tent that had been furnished her and Captain Hunt and stole her trunk, with nearly all of her clothes and some $5,000 in greenbacks that were in the trunk." He felt pity that her child was kept warm by pieces of cloth ripped off of her dress.

In the same article, Kerr wrote that he went back to his office and wrote out a "petition to General [John Henry] Winder." All of the post surgeons signed the petition to the general. The original petition was to have Janie Hunt and her infant immediately taken out of the prison and given a room in a resident's home outside the prison. Dr. Kerr was flabbergasted that General Winder knew that Janie was there with her husband. Brigadier General Winder stated, "It would be against the rules of war to board her out, though he would like to do so if he could." After Kerr pleaded with Winder, the general finally relented and told Kerr that if he could find suitable quarters outside the camp, he would pretend he knew nothing of it.

The doctor moved quickly, traveling outside the camp and talking to local residents. He recollected that a farmer by the name of Smith agreed to house the infant and Janie Hunt. They needed more than room and board. Kerr wrote that both mother and child needed to secure bare essentials. The Smiths could not be expected to furnish these articles. Dr. Kerr remembered that he had a friend who owned a general store in Macon, Georgia. Once again, the doctor was able to secure essentials from his friend in Macon. When he returned to Andersonville, he had it all sent to Janie to make her more comfortable. Janie became concerned about repaying the doctor for all his kindness. When she saw her husband, she asked him for his scarf pin with diamonds set in it. The couple offered it to Kerr as a gift, but he refused to take it.

Dr. Kerr's acts of kindness were not done yet. He worked behind the scenes to have Captain Hunt paroled. After all, he wished for the father to see his son and survive the hellish conditions of Andersonville Prison. Kerr "had him appointed ward master in the hospital so he could go be with his wife." A short time after this transpired, an urgent plea came from the captain for Dr. Kerr to go to the home where his wife stayed. Their son, Harry Jr., was very sick and needed medical attention. Kerr told years later that he saw through the ruse. The child was not sick. The couple wanted to make sure that Kerr would allow them to repay his kindness with the scarf-pin that the doctor had refused to take. He did finally take the pin because he did not want to insult Mr. and Mrs. Hunt. Janie told him to wear it as long as he lived.

Eventually, Capt. Harry Hunt, Janie, and Harry Jr. left the South when Andersonville no longer served a function as the war came to an end in April 1865. In his article for the *Confederate Veteran*, Dr. W. J. W. Kerr wrote, "I have tried every way imaginable to find Captain Harry Hunt or his wife, but have been unable to do so." He concluded with a plea to the readers, "If any one can give me information of them, I would be glad indeed."

Recently, Robert Scott Davis, in his book on Andersonville Prison, debunked the story that has been told by Dr. Kerr. He believes it is off on many levels. Davis surmises that the inconsistencies in Kerr's story might have something to do with why he could not find the couple.

Davis does not dispute the fact that Janie had a child at Andersonville Prison. However, he writes in his book, *Ghosts and Shadows of Ander-*

sonville: Essay on the Secret Social Histories of America's Deadliest Prison, that Kerr remembered the event almost five decades later. Much of the story he asserts was at best third-hand.

According to Davis, Harry Hunt was Herbert Hunt of Buffalo. He was not born in Buffalo, New York, but in Maine on December 25, 1838.

Furthermore, he did not work out of New York City, but "on the Hudson/Erie Canal/Great Lakes/ Mississippi network." In Chicago, he met Francis Jane "Fannie" "Janie" Scadden, who was born in Michigan four years after her future husband. Her father was not Thomas L. Scadden, but Robert.

When Dr. Kerr found the couple "living outside the Andersonville Stockade," they "had a 3-day old child referred to as 'little Harry.'" In Davis's version the child's name was Frank, and the couple had already been married some two years when the child had been born. They probably were not married in New York City, but quite possibly Chicago. In fact, Herbert had been in the Union army, enlisting in 1861 with the 61st Illinois Infantry regiment, and discharged in 1862 for medical reasons.

After being released from the prison in April 1865, they eventually ended up in New Jersey with many children born to the couple. It is believed that the child born at Andersonville died before the Hunts were paroled. After living in New Jersey, Davis tracked the Hunts down to Rocky Hill, Connecticut, where Jane died in 1894 and Herbert in 1926. Thus, the story of the only child born in Andersonville Prison came to an end. There is no proof that Janie Hunt dressed as a male soldier to avoid detection.

As in every war, some families were left wondering whatever became of their son or daughter. Sometimes, the military had no information other than the person was lost. Families were left to grieve over the family member's loss, and the fact there were no remains to bury led them to cling to a false hope that their loved one would walk through the door of their home one day. These are some of the most upsetting casualties. Many soldiers could not be accounted for or identified because their wounds were so grievous, and women soldiers were no exception. Some died as unknowns in battle, as well as in prisoner of war camps.

There is a woman buried in the Andersonville National Cemetery who is an "unknown." There were women soldiers in the Union army captured by Confederate troops and able to keep their identity a secret. If they were found out, many times they were paroled out to the North for their safety, and as previously stated, women in the military were illegal as was dressing as a man. The woman soldier forever named "Unknown" was able to keep her identity quiet until her death. She did use an alias, but that has been lost to time.

Her story is told by another woman soldier named Madame Collier. She was a Union soldier and captured by Confederate forces. After her capture, she was sent to Belle Isle Prison in Richmond, Virginia. Various versions of the story exist about how Collier's identity was discovered. Some speculate that she might have confided in a fellow soldier who betrayed Collier. Still, other researchers assert that she was found out. Once discovered, historian Marlea S. Donaho argues in her thesis, "Belle Isle, Point Lookout, the Press, and the Government: The Press and Reality of Civil War Prison Camps" that Madame Collier might have been an alias to protect her identity. Collier claimed that she dressed as a man to enlist with a man she loved.

After being discovered, Collier was sent north to be paroled back to the Union lines. Once back and settled, she reported that she was not the only woman disguised as a man. She recounted the story of how and where she met the woman referred to as Unknown. In February 1864, because of attacks on Richmond, prisoners of war were sent to Georgia to the new prison Andersonville. The woman that Collier met at Belle probably was sent to Andersonville. Donaho also notes that Collier mentioned a parentless sixteen-year-old named Mary Jane Johnson and postulates that this might have been the name of the woman she was referencing as Unknown.

No one knows for sure what became of this "unknown" woman in Andersonville. Her "disguise" was never betrayed. She did die before Andersonville was closed at the end of the Civil War in April 1865. It is in death that her secret was revealed. Some hypothesize that her clothing was taken from her in death because it was in short supply in the prison camp. No one knew her real name, and it was decided to leave her unidentified. As Larry G. Eggleston wrote in *Women in the Civil War: Extraordinary Stories of Soldiers, Spies, Nurses, Doctors, Crusaders, and Others*, maybe one day, through modern methods and research, we will be able to find out not only how she died, but also her identity.

According to Alton in the Civil War, "the Alton prison opened in 1833 as the first Illinois State Penitentiary and was closed in 1860 when the last prisoners were moved to a new facility at Joliet. By late in 1861, an urgent need arose to relieve the overcrowding at 2 St. Louis prisons. On December 31, 1861, Major General Henry Halleck, Commander of the Department of the Missouri, ordered Lieutenant-Colonel James B. McPherson to Alton to inspect the closed penitentiary. Colonel McPherson reported that the prison could be made into a military prison and house up to 1,750 prisoners with improvements estimated to cost $2,415." According to a 1909 article in a Colorado newspaper, one of the Confederate prisoners of war in 1863 was B. A. Duravan.

In an article published widely, including in the *New York Herald* in 1909, an old citizen remembered her story when a memorial was erected for Confederate veterans who died while imprisoned. This unnamed gentleman remembered that a small and frail soldier was part of a large contingent of prisoners that were transferred to Alton. When he was asked his name, the skeleton of a man responded B. A. Duravan. This elderly gentleman speaking to the *New York Herald* stated that this frail soldier named Duravan had been "where the bullets were flying thick and fast." He had also marched with Robert E. Lee's Army of Northern Virginia. All that he used to keep warm sometimes was the ground or a blanket of snow. The story noted that "Comrades have a warm spot in their hearts for Duravan," who firmly believed in the cause of the South and the defeat of the Union.

In 1909, the newspaper was running the story because a tablet was being erected in Alton for the Confederate soldiers who had been kept as prisoners and died in the smallpox epidemic of 1863. According to this story, a Confederate spy was apprehended by the name of B. A. Duravan. Some of the other Confederates, such as Thomas Pinckney, suspected that Duravan could be a woman. However, they did not have any proof. According to Alton's history, Alton suffered from many of the same scourges as other prisons. The soldiers exceedingly feared smallpox, which in the winter of 1862 began to spread through the prison. The only way to contain it was to quarantine those believed to have it or exposed to it. Those believed to have it moved to an island in the Mississippi River where a quarantine hospital was located. B. A. Duravan contracted smallpox, and was moved to the island. He would not survive the virus. On September 23, 1863, he was found dead in his cell. In death, his secret came to light. B. A. Duravan was Barbara A. Duravan of Tennessee.

Over a thousand Confederates died while imprisoned in Alton. They were buried on Smallpox Island in the Mississippi River. This island eventually was flooded and covered by the river, and the graves were lost. In 1909, a monument was erected at the Mississippi's water edge, with a plaque to the memory of those Confederates who died and their graves lost.

When those interested in the Civil War were looking for evidence of women who served as soldiers during the Civil War, newspapers reporting on Duravan elevated her to the level of a soldier and spy who rode with Robert E. Lee's Army of Northern Virginia. Those that were looking for a hero in Duravan have found out that 140 years later, they are a step closer to knowing who she might have been. The authors of *They Fought Like Demons* found in their research at the National Archives that Barbara A. Duravan, was in "reality poor and illiterate." She was from Tennessee and "was court-martialed for smuggling revolvers to the Confederate army."

Catherine E. Davidson was in love. She lived in Sheffield, Ohio, and intended to marry her fiancé—but then the Civil War started. She decided to dress as a man and join him in the 28th Ohio Infantry; they planned on postponing their marrage until after the war. This, however, would not be. During the Battle of Antietam, her fiancé was shot dead while Catherine was shot in the arm. Jim Murphy, in his book *A Savage Thunder*, states that "She was helped into a ambulance by the Governor of Pennsylvania, Andrew Gregg Curtin." Curtin had no idea that the private with a horrible arm wound was a woman.

Probably in shock from loss of blood and pain, Davidson took off her ring and gave it to the governor. She told him that she was dying and that it was all she had to repay his kindness. When she arrived before the surgeon, her arm was amputated. After having time to recover, she left the army and shed her male persona. Having been told who saved her life, she went to visit the governor.

According to newspaper reporting on the incident in 1863, the governor was at the Continental Hotel in Philadelphia. "When she was introduced into the parlor, she expressed her great joy at seeing the Governor, at the same time imprinting a kiss upon his forehead." When he asked who she was, Davidson recounted the entire incident, even the governor's ring which at that moment he was wearing. She pointed out her initials inside the ring.

Perplexed, the governor tried to figure out who she was and how she knew about the ring. He asked her if the soldier he helped was her loved one? In *Rifle Shots and Bugle Notes*, the authors write that she stated, "'I loved him as I loved my life, but he never returned that love. He had more love for his country than me. I honor him for it. That soldier who placed that ring upon your finger stands before you.'" Davidson was not the only woman fighting at Antietam. It is believed that around eight women fought during that bloody battle.

There was yet another woman who served at Antietam who was not found out as a woman until after being honorably discharged. On August 25, 1863, the *Courier-Journal* of Louisville, Kentucky, reported that "In Harrisburg, on Friday a discharged soldier who had been living rather high for several days was arrested on suspicion of being a female." When interrogated, she confessed that she was from Rochester, New York, and her real name was Ida Remington. What her alias was in the 11th New York Militia is not stated. When asked what brought her to Harrisburg, she exclaimed that her regiment was in the area. Remington explained that she had enlisted about two years earlier and mostly was a servant for a captain.

When pressed for more of her story, Ida told the police that with the 11th, she had been at the battles of South Mountain, Antietam, and "many other hard-fought battles, and had with her an honorable discharge from the service." She was still jailed but released after a second hearing. When asked why she joined the 11th New York Militia, she retorted that some friends convinced her to do it. Like so many of the women who served in the Civil War, Ida vanished into obscurity.

These women all had unfinished lives either because their husbands, beaus, or they themselves died, never allowing them that chance to find a fulfilling life. Some did not die but were horribly disfigured by injuries, which limited their futures. One woman died in battle while pregnant, with her fetus meeting the same fate. Finally the unknowns, who struggled and died only to not even be remembered, are perhaps the epitome of the unfinished life.

Bibliography

GENERAL RESOURCES

Adams, George Worthington. *Doctors in Blue: The Medical History of the Union Army in the Civil War*. Baton Rouge: Louisiana State University Press, 1950.

Blanton, DeAnne. "Women Soldiers of the Civil War." *Prologue*, Spring 1993.

Blanton, DeAnne, and Lauren M. Cook. *They Fought Like Demons: Women Soldiers in the Civil War*. Baton Rouge: Louisiana State University Press, 2002.

Eggleston, Larry G. *Women in the Civil War: Extraordinary Stories of Soldiers, Spies, Nurses, Doctors, Crusaders, and Others*. Jefferson, NC: McFarland and Company, 2003.

Keeler, Alonzo M. *A Guest of the Confederacy: The Civil War Letters and Diaries of Alonzo M. Keeler, Captain, Company B, Twenty-Second Michigan Infantry*. Eds. Robert D. and Cheryl J. Allen. Nashville, TN: Cold Tree Press, 2008.

McPherson, James M. *Battle Cry of Freedom*. New York: Oxford University Press, 1988.

McPherson, James M. *Crossroads of Freedom: Antietam*. New York: Oxford University Press, 2002.

McPherson, James M. *For Causes and Comrades: Why Men Fought in the Civil War*. New York: Oxford University Press, 1997.

Newton, James K. *A Wisconsin Boy in Dixie: The Civil War Letters of James K. Newton*. Ed. Stephen E. Ambrose. Madison: University of Wisconsin Press, 1961.

Pryor, Elizabeth Brown. *Clara Barton: Professional Angel*. Philadelphia: University of Pennsylvania Press, 1987.

Rhodes, Elisha Hunt. *All for the Union: The Civil War Diary and Letters of Elisha Hunt Rhodes*. Ed. Robert Hunt Rhodes. New York: Vintage Books, 1992.

Wakeman, Sarah Rosetta. *An Uncommon Soldier: The Civil War Letters of Sarah Rosetta Wakeman*. Ed. Lauren Cook Burgess. New York: Oxford University Press, 1994.

Watkins, Sam R. *"Co. Aytch," Maury Grays, First Tennessee Regiment: Or, A Side Show of the Big Show*. New York: Plume, 1999.

Wiley, Bell Irvin. *The Life of Billy Yank: The Common Soldier of the Union Bell*. Baton Rouge: Louisiana State University Press, 1971.

JOHNNY CLEM (THE DRUMMER BOY OF CHICKAMAUGA)

"Career of a Drummer Boy." *Fort Scott Republican*, February 19, 1913.

"Civil War Boy Turns 84." *Semi-Weekly Spokesman Review*, August 13, 1935.

Clem Letters. Licking County Historical Society. Licking County, Ohio.

Cohasey, John. *The 22nd Michigan Infantry and the Road to Chickamauga.* Jefferson, NC: McFarland & Company, 2019.

Cozens, Peter. *The Battle of Chickamauga: The Terrible Sound.* Urbana: University of Illinois Press, 1996.

Daily Milwaukee News, December 17, 1863.

Daily Sentinel, September 9, 1895.

"Drummer Boy of Chickamauga: Retired Major General Clem Dies at San Antonio Home." *Denton Record Chronicle*, May 14, 1937.

"Famed Drummer of Chickamauga John L. Clem Dies at San Antonio." *Big Spring Daily Herald*, May 14, 1937.

Grant, U.S. RG94 Letter of May 8, 1869 from U.S. Rep John A Logan of Illinois to U.S. Grant. *The Papers of Ulysses S. Grant Digital Edition.* Charlottesville Record Group 94, Virginia: University of Virginia Press Rotunda, 2018.

Historical Collections of Ohio in Two Volumes. Ed. Henry Howe LLD. Cincinnati, OH: C.J. Krehbiel & Co., 1907.

Illinois Department of Public Health, Division of Vital Records. John L. Clem Death Certificate.

"John Clem in Civil War at 10." *Star Press*, August 8, 1909.

"Johnny Clem To Be Visitor." *Chattanooga Daily Times*, August 6, 1923.

Mattingly, Herman E. "The Family of 'Johnny' Clem Drummer Boy of Chickamauga." *Catholic Record Society Bulletin*, July 1976.

"Obituary for Roman Klem." *Newark Daily Advocate*, November 17, 1890.

"Only Civil War Veteran in Our Army To Be Retired Soon." *New York Times*, June 21, 1914.

The Outlook, May–August 1914.

Record of Service of Michigan Volunteers in the Civil War 1861–65. Michigan Adjutant General's Office. Ed. George H. Turner. Kalamazoo, MI: Ihling Bros & Everard, 1905.

Records of the Adjutant General's Office, 1762–1984. "Compiled Military Service Record John Klem." Record Group 94. National Archives, Washington, DC.

Shiloh and the Western Campaign of 1862. Eds. O. Edward Cunningham, Gary D. Joiner, and Timothy Smith. New York: Savis Beatie, 2009.

"Ten-Year Old Boy Was a Soldier." *Boston Globe*, March 9, 1913.

"Then Blue and Gray Fought Without Hate 'Little' Johnny Clem's Story." *Lansing State Journal*, May 31, 1915.

"The War Day by Day." *Washington Herald*, March 22, 1914.

US Bureau of the Census of Population. "11th Census of U.S. Special Schedule Surviving Soldiers, Sailors and Marine and Widows, etc of the Civil War." Washington, DC: Government Printing Office, 1890.

US Bureau of the Census of Population. Washington, DC: Government Printing Office, 1910.

US Bureau of the Census of Population. Washington, DC: Government Printing Office, 1920.

US Bureau of the Census of Population. Washington, DC: Government Printing Office, 1930.

SUSIE KING TAYLOR (NURSE AND TEACHER)

Ash, Stephen V. Firebrand of Liberty: The Story of Two Black Regiments That Changed theCourse of the Civil War. New York: W.W. Norton, 2008.

Butchart, Ronald E. "Susie King Taylor (1848–1912)." Accessed 10/29/2020. www.Georgiaencyclopedia.org/articles/history-archaeology/Susie-king-taylor -1846-1912.

Death Certificate Mass Vital Records, 1840–1911. New England Genealogical Society, Boston, Massachusetts.

Dyer, Frederic, A. A Compendium of the War of the Rebellion. Vol. 4, Series 2. Des Moines, IA: The Dyer Publishing Company, 1908.

Espiritu, Allison. "Susan Taylor (Susie) Baker King (1848–1912)." Accessed 10/29/2020. www.Blackpast.org/african-american-history/taylor-susan-susie -baker-king-1848-1912.

Florida History Online. "Wartime Letters from Seth Rogers M.D. Surgeon of the 1st S.C. Afterward the 33rd United States Colored Troops 1862-1863. 10/29/2020. https://www.unf.edu/floridahistoryonline/Projects/Rogers /index.html.

The Georgia Archives. "County Marriage Records, 1828–1878." Marrow, Georgia.

Georgia Women Their Lives and Times. Eds. Ann Short Chirhart and Betty Wood. Vol. 1. Athens: University of Georgia Press, 2009.

Higginson, Thomas Wentworth. Army Life in a Black Regiment. Boston: Field, Osgood & Co., 1870.

National Park Service. "Susie King Taylor." Accessed 10/29/2020. www.nps.gov/people /susie-king-taylor.htm.

Oates, Stephen B. A Woman of Valor: Clara Barton and the Civil War. New York: The Free Press, 1994.

Taylor, Susie King. Reminiscences of My Life in Camp with the 33d U.S. Colored Troops Late 1st South Carolina Volunteers. Boston: NP, 1902.

US Bureau of the Census of Population. Washington, DC: Government Printing Office, 1880.

US Bureau of the Census of Population. Washington, DC: Government Printing Office, 1900.

US Bureau of the Census of Population. Washington, DC: Government Printing Office, 1910.

US War Department. The War of the Rebellion: A Compilation of the Official Records of the Union and Confederate Armies. Series I, Vol. 14. Washington, DC: Government Printing Office, 1880–1901.

US War Department. *The War of the Rebellion: A Compilation of the Official Records of the Union and Confederate Armies.* Vol. 28, Part 1. Washington, DC: Government Printing Office, 1880–1901.

CHARLES WHIPPLE HADLEY (BRAVERY AT SHILOH)

Catton, Bruce. "Grant at Shiloh." *American Heritage*, February 1960.

Charles Whipple Hadley, Civil War and Later Pension Files; Department of Veterans Affairs, Record Group 15; National Archives, Washington, DC.

Charles Whipple Hadley Diary, MSS177 Folder 2. Tom Perry Special Collections, Harold B. Lee Library, Brigham Young University.

"Invalid G.A.R. Slays Self with Gun." *Salt Lake Tribune*, July 21, 1936.

Parsons, Elizabeth. *Fearless Purpose: Memoir of Emily Elizabeth Parsons*. New York: Little Brown and Company, 1880.

Pickenpaugh, Roger. *Captives in Blue: The Civil War Prisons of the Confederacy*. Tuscaloosa: University of Alabama Press, 2013.

Reed, D. W. *The Battle of Shiloh*. Washington, DC: Government Printing Office, 1913.

State Historical Society of Iowa. "College Student and Soldier Boy." Summer 1944.

US Bureau of the Census of Population. Washington, DC: Government Printing Office, 1900.

US Bureau of the Census of Population. Washington, DC: Government Printing Office, 1910.

US Bureau of the Census of Population. Washington, DC: Government Printing Office, 1920.

US Bureau of the Census of Population. Washington, DC: Government Printing Office, 1930.

Utah State Archives. "Certificate of Death Series 181448." Salt Lake City, Utah.

THE HOWE BROTHERS (ORION AND LYSTON)

The American Medical Dictionary. Boston: Houghton Mifflin Co., 2008.

Andrus, Onley. *The Civil War Letters of Sergeant Onley Andrus*. Ed. Fred Albert Shannon. Urbana, Chicago: University of Illinois, 1947.

Brown, J. G. H. S. Nourse, and Lucin Bonaparte. *The Story of the Fifty-Fifth Regiment Illinois Volunteer Infantry in the Civil War 1861–65*. Clinton, MA: W. J. Coulter, 1887.

Committee of the Regiment. *The Story of the 55th Illinois Infantry in the Civil War 1861–65*. Clinton, MA: W. J. Coulter, 1887.

"Dr. O.P. Howe Honored by His Captain." *Hill City Republican*, June 11, 1911.

Edwards, Josh. "The First Assault on Town Broke Spirit of Union Troops." Accessed 4/8/2020. www.vicksburgpost.com/2015/05/20/first-sualt-on-town-broke-spirit-of-union-troops.

Email with Janey Bunde, Archivist New York University Special Collections, November 11, 2019.

Illinois History Lincoln Collections. "Jonathan Catlin 52nd Illinois Vol. Infantry Regiment." Accessed 4/18/2020. https://publishillinois.edu/in/c-blog/2018/07 /16jonathan-caitlin-52nd-illinois-volunteers-infantry-regiment/.

Kroff, Charles. *Diary of Charles Kroff Co. F 11th Indiana Infantry Volunteers.* Accessed 10/30/2020. https://digital.libraries.ou.edu/cdm/singleitem/collection/Cresis/8.

Lincoln, Abraham. "Proclamation By the President Calling Up the Militia April 15, 1861." Robert Todd Lincoln Papers, Manuscript Division, Library of Congress, Washington, DC.

"Lyston Howe Contributed Invention of Coal Washer." *Streator Times,* June 29, 1976.

"Lyston Separated from His Company." *Streator Times,* 1958.

Murphy, Jim. *The Boys' War: Confederate and Union Soldiers Talk About the Civil War.* New York: Scholastic, 1990.

National Park Service. "Shiloh Battlefield-Hornet's Nest." Accessed 4/8/2020. www.nps.gov/places/shiloh-battlefield-hornets-nest.htm.

Newton, James K. A Wisconsin Boy in Dixie: Civil War Letters of James K. Newton. Ed. Stephen E. Ambrose. Madison: University of Wisconsin Press, 1961.

Orion Howe, Civil War and Later Pension Files; Department of Veterans Affairs, Record Group 15; National Archives, Washington, DC.

Sherman, William T. Memoirs of General William T. Sherman. New York: P. Appleton and Co., 1913.

Sigalas, Mike. Vicksburg: A Guided Tour through History. Guilford, CT: Globe Pequot Press, 2010.

"Small Boots: Big Man—Lyston Howe, Union Soldier." *The Times-Press,* Streator, June 22, 1968.

Soldiers and Patriots Biographical Album. Chicago: Union Veteran Publishing Co., 1892.

Stanley, Charles. "Howe Brothers Focus of Civil War Memorial." *The Times Streator,* May 23, 2009.

"Streator Man Holds an Honor." *The Times Streator,* July 18, 1906.

Stockwell, Elisha, Jr. Private Elisha Stockwell, Jr. Sees the Civil War. Ed. Byron R. Abernathy. Norman: University of Oklahoma Press, 1968.

"Story Told by Captain." *Streator Free Press,* May 13, 1909.

Walton, Clyde C. *Illinois in the Civil War.* Chicago: State of Illinois, 1962.

"Wife Seeks Relief for Battle Hero." *Buffalo Sunday Morning News,* August 25, 1912.

Winschel, Terrence J. "The Key to Victory: An Overview of the Vicksburg Campaign." Accessed 11/10/2020. http://nphistory/series/symposia/gettysburg_seminars/8 /essay3.pdf 4/8/2020.

Winschel, Terrence J. *Vicksburg: Fall of the Confederate Gibraltar.* Abilene, TX: McWhiney Foundation Press, 1999.

WILLIAM H. HORSFALL (MEDAL OF HONOR)

Adjutant General of the State of Kentucky. *Report of the Adjutant General of the State of Kentucky (*1861–1866). Vol. 1. Frankfort, KY: John H. Harney, 1866.

Campbell County Historical Society. *William H. Horsfall Family Files.*

"Civil War Hero Dies." *Cincinnati Enquirer*, October 24, 1922.
The Encyclopedia of Northern Kentucky. Eds. Paul A. Tenkot and James C. Claypool. Lexington: University Press of Kentucky, 2009.
Fiore, C. A. *Young Heroes of the Civil War*. Unionville, NY: Royal Works Press, 1932.
The Messenger (Madisonville, Kentucky), December 1, 1996.
News-Democrat (Paducah, Kentucky), October 24, 1922.
"Obituary of WH Horsfall." *Kentucky Times-Star*, October 25, 1922.
Prittle, Alfred. *The Union Regiments of Kentucky Capt. Thos Speed, Col R.M. Kelly*. Louisville, KY: Alfred Prittle, 1897.
Records of the Adjutant General's Office, 1762–1984. "Compiled Military Service Record William H. Horsfall." Record Group 94. National Archives, Washington, DC.
Richmond Register, November 12, 2013.
Speed, Thomas. *The Union Cause in Kentucky 1860–1865*. New York: GP Putnam's Sons, 1907.
US War Department. *The War of the Rebellion: A Compilation of the Official Records of the Union and Confederate Armies*. Series 1, Volume 10, Chapter 22, Part II. Washington, DC: Government Printing Office, 1880–1901.
William H. Horsfall, Civil War and Later Pension Files; Department of Veterans Affairs, Record Group 15; National Archives, Washington, DC.

ALEXANDER H. JOHNSON (DRUMMER FOR THE 54TH)

Battle of Olustee. Accessed 11/2/2020. www.battleofolustee.org/pics/alexander_john son.html.
Coddington, R. S. *African American Faces of the Civil War: An Album*. Baltimore: The Johns Hopkins University Press, 2012.
Coddington, Ronald S. "The Legacy of the Shaw Memorial Is a Steady Drumbeat of Hope." Accessed 11/2/2020. https://www.press.jhu/news/blog/legacy-shaw -memorial-steady-drumbeat-hope.
Emilio, Luis F. History of the Fifty-Fourth Regiment of Massachusetts Volunteer Infantry 1863–1865. Boston: The Boston Book Co., 1894.
"55th Anniversary of the Event To Be Celebrated by S of V." Boston Globe, July 7, 1918.
Gooding, James Henry. On the Altar of Freedom: A Black Soldier's Civil War Letters from the Front. Ed. Virginia M. Adams. Boston: University of Massachusetts, 1999.
Kentake, Meserette. "Alexander H. Johnson: The First Drummer Boy." Accessed 11/2/2020. https://kentakepage.com/alexander-j-johnson-the-first-drummer -boy/.
Massachusetts Soldiers, Sailors and Marines in the Civil War, Vol. IV. Ed. Adjutant General of Massachusetts. Norwood, MA: Norwood Press, 1932.
Moore, Arthur J. "The Original Drummer Boy." Accessed 11/2/2020. www.acrossthe valleytodarkness.com.

New Bedford Historical Society. "The 54th Regiment: Men of Color to Arms."
    Accessed 11/2/2020. http://nbhistoricalsociety.org/.
Records of the Office of Quartermaster General. "Application for Headstones for
    United States Military Veterans, 1925–1941"; Record Group No. 92. National
    Archives, Washington, DC.
Sneade, David "Chet" Williamson. "The Rhythm of the 54th." Jazz Riffing on a Lost
    Worcester. Accessed 11/3/2020. http://jazzriffing.blogspot.com/2016/01/the
    -rhythm-of-54th.html.
Springfield (MA) Republican, March 27, 1930.
US Bureau of the Census of Population. Washington, DC: Government Printing
    Office, 1880.
US Bureau of the Census of Population. Washington, DC: Government Printing
    Office, 1900.
US Bureau of the Census of Population. Washington, DC: Government Printing
    Office, 1910.
US Bureau of the Census of Population. Washington, DC: Government Printing
    Office, 1920.
"Worcester Rotary Club Entertains Veterans." *Boston Globe*, May 28, 1926.

LOLA SANCHEZ (CONFEDERATE SPY)

Caban, Pedro, Barbara Cruz, and Jose Carrasco. *The Latino Experince in United States
    History.* New York: Globe Pearson, 1994.
Chisolm, William D. "True Heroine for the Confederacy To Be Honored." *Columbia
    (SC) Star*, 2008.
Confederate Veteran, August 1909, Vol. 17.
Connecticut Adjutant-General's Office. *The First Regiment, Connecticut Volunteer Heavy
    Artillery in the War of the Rebellion, 1861–1865.* Hartford, CT: Lockwood &
    Brainard, 1889.
Cuevas, Rebecca, M. "Hispanic Confederate Heritage—The Sanchez Sister." Accessed
    11/2/2020. www.bellaonline.com/articles/art/art40197.asp.
Eggleston, Larry G. *Women in the Civil War: Extraordinary Stories of Soldiers, Spies,
    Nurses, Doctors, Crusaders, and Others.* Jefferson, NC: McFarland and Company,
    2003.
Frank, Lisa. *Women in the American Civil War Vol. I.* Santa Barbara, CA: ABC-Clio,
    2008.
Gladwin, William J., Jr. "Men, Salt, Cattle and Battle: The Civil War in Florida
    (November 1860–July 1865)." Newport, RI: Naval War College, 1992.
The Historical Marker Database. "The Battle at Horse Landing." Accessed November 2,
    2020. https://www.hmdb.org/m.asp?m=101762.
Underwood, J. L. *The Women of the Confederacy.* New York: Neale Publishing, 1906.
Women in Civil War Texas. Eds. Deborah M. Liles and Angela Boswell. Denton: Uni-
    versity of North Texas Press, 2016.

UNFINISHED LIVES, PART I

Bailey, A. *Bailey's Indianapolis Directory 1871-72*. Indianapolis, IN: A. Bailey, 1872.

Black, George H. *Discharge*. Indiana State Archives and Records Administration.

"Charley King's Civil War Drum Career." Accessed 7/4/2020. www.main-line-history
-charleykings-civil-war-drum-career/.

Children's Museum of Indianapolis. "Edward Black Drum." Accessed 10/28/2020.
http://thehistorychildrensmuseum.org/collections/iconic-objects/edward-black
-drum.

"Clarence D. McKenzie." *Brooklyn Eagle*, June 15, 1861.

Confederate States Army Casualties: Lists and Narrative Reports, 1861–1865. Records of
the Adjutant and Inspector General's Department. War Department Collection
of Confederate Records, Record Group 15. National Archives, Washington, DC.

Edward Black, Case Files of Approved Pension Files; Department of Veterans Affairs,
Record Group 15; National Archives, Washington, DC.

Evening News (Indianapolis, Indiana), July 1, 1871.

Friends of Memory Cemetery. Accessed 9/2/2020. http://friendsofcems.org/memory
hill/MoreInfo.php?888EF026008.

HistoryNet. "America's Civil War: Where Does Private Jemison Rest?" Accessed
9/2/2020. https://www.historynet.com/americas-civil-war-where-does-private
-jemison-rest.htm.

Horowitz, Tony. "Did Civil War Soldiers Have PTSD." *Smithsonian Magazine*.
Accessed 10/28/2020. https://www.smithsonianmag.com/history/ptsd-civil
-wars-hidden-legacy-180953652/.

Indiana Digital Archives. "Find Your Ancestors." Accessed 7/4/2020. https://secure
.in.gov/apps/iara/search/.

Indiana State Archives. Graves Registration Form No.1, The American Legion, Indiana
State Archives.

Indiana State Archives. Indiana Archives and Records Administration. "Indiana
Volunteers."

Johnstone, Malcolm. "Westchester History: The Youngest Soldiers To Die in Battle."
Accessed 10/28/2020. www.downtownwestchester.com/view-program.php?id
=446.

Love, William DeLoss. *Wisconsin in the War of the Rebellion*. Chicago: Church and
Goodman, 1866.

Moore, Arthur J. "Journey into Darkness: A Story in Four Parts." Accessed 10/28/2020.
www.acrossthevalleyintodarkness.com/.

Murphy, Jim. *The Boys' War: Confederate and Union Soldiers Talk About the Civil War*.
New York: Scholastic, 1990.

National Archives. Index to Compiled Service Records of Volunteer Union Soldiers
Who Served in Organizations from the State of Wisconsin. Record Group 94.
National Archives, Washington, DC.

National Archives. *Indiana in the Civil War, ICPR Digital Archives Accession Number
1938004 Edward Black*, Indiana State Archives, Indiana Archives and Records
Administration, Indianapolis, Indiana.

The National Cemetery Administration. "Burial Ledgers." Record Group 15. National Archives, Washington, DC.

National Park Service. "Andersonville, Georgia Andersonville Prisoner of War Database." Accessed 10/28/2020. https://www.nps.gov/civilwar/search-prisoners.htm.

National Park Service. "Battle of Malvern Hill." Accessed 9/3/2020. https://www.battle fields.org/learn/civil-war/battles/malvern-hill.

National Park Service. "The Civil War's Common Soldier." Accessed 7/4/2020. www .nps.gov/parkhistory/online_books/civil_war_series/3/sec1.htm accessed.

National Park Service. "Search Battle Units." Accessed 9/3/2020. https://www.nps.gov /civilwar/search-battle-units-detail.htm?battleUnitCode=CLA0002RI.

National Park Service. "Union Wisconsin Volunteers." Accessed 10/28/2020. www.nps .gov/civilwar/search-battle-units-details.htm?battleunitcode=UW10007Rl.

New York State Archives, Cultural Education Center, Albany, New York: NY Civil War Muster Roll Abstracts, 1861–1900. Box #667, Roll #323.

New York State Archives, Albany, New York. NY Civil War Muster Roll Abstracts, 1861–1900. Box #694, Roll #350.

New York State Archives, New York, New York. Town Clerks' Registers of Men Who Served in the Civil War ca. 1861–65. Box #12, Roll # 8.

New York State Bureau of Military Statistics. Registers of Officers and Enlisted Men Mustered into Federal Military or Naval Service During the Civil War, 6 vols. Albany, New York: New York State Archives.

Ouachita Telegraph (Monroe, Louisiana), January 1, 1887.

Obituary of Edward Black, Indiana State Archives, Indiana Archives and Records Administration. Indianapolis, Indiana.

Personal Recollections of the War of the Rebellion Military of the Rebellion: Address Delivered Before the Commandery of the State of New York. Military Order of the Loyal Legion of the United States New York Commander. Ed. A. Noel Blakeman. New York: G. P. Putnam & Sons, 1912, 4th series.

Public Broadcasting Service. "Kids in the Civil War." Accessed 9/3/2020. https://www .pbs.org/wgbh/americanexperience/features/grant-kids/.

Rashio Crane. *General Index to Pensions 1861–1934.* Record Group 15. National Archives, Washington, DC.

Records of the Office of the Quartermaster General 1774–1985. Internment Control Forms 1928–1962. Record Group 92. National Archives, College Park, Maryland.

Report of the Adjutant General of the State of Indiana 1861–65, Vol. II. Indianapolis, IN: W.B. Holloway, StatePrinter, 1866.

Report of the Adjutant General of the State of Indiana. 1861–65, Vol. IV. Indianapolis, IN: Samuel M. Douglas, State Printer, 1866.

Sketches of the War History, 1861–1865: Papers Read Before the Ohio Commandery of the Military Order of the Loyal Legion of the United States, Vol. 6. Eds. Theodore F. Allen et al. Cincinnati, OH: R. Clarke & Co., 1908.

Southern Recorder, August 5, 1862.

State of Ohio Roster Commission (1886–1895). *Official Roster of the Soldiers of the State of Ohio in the War of the Rebellion, 1861–1866.* Vol. 1. Akron: Werner Co., 1893.

US Bureau of the Census of Population. Washington, DC: Government Printing Office, 1850.

US Bureau of the Census of Population. Washington, DC: Government Printing Office, 1860.

US Bureau of the Census of Population. Washington, DC: Government Printing Office, 1870.

Village Record, October 2, 1862.

Village Record, December 31, 1861.

Wasie, Andy. "Charles 'Charley' King." Accessed 7/4/2020. www.pacivilwar150.com /throughpeople/children/charlescharleyking.html.

Werner, Emmy E. *Reluctant Witnesses: Children's Voices from the Civil War.* Boulder, CO: Westview Press, 1998.

Westbrook, Robert S. *History of the 49th Pennsylvania Volunteers.* Altoona, PA: Altoona Times, 1898.

Wiley, Bell Irvin. *The Life of Johnny Reb: The Common Soldier of the Confederacy.* Baton Rouge: Louisiana State University Press, 2008.

ALBERT D. J. CASHIER (JENNIE HODGERS)

"Albert Cashier Is Dead: Fought as Man." *Muscatine Journal,* October 12, 1915.

Albert D. J. Cashier, Civil War and Later Pension Files; Department of Veterans Affairs, Record

Group 15; National Archives, Washington, DC.

Andrus, Onley. *The Civil War Letters of Sergeant Onley Andrus.* Ed. Fred Albert Shannon. Urbana: University of Illinois Press, 1947.

Blanton, DeAnne, and Lauren M. Cook. *They Fought Like Demons: Women Soldiers in the Civil War.* Baton Rouge: Louisiana State University Press, 2002.

"Civil War Centennial Brings Albert To Mind." *The Pantagraph,* May 30, 1962.

"Civil War Letters of Amory K. Allen." *Indiana Magazine of History,* December 1935.

Databases of Illinois Veterans, Illinois State Archive. Accessed 11/10/2020. https:// www.cyberdriveillinois.com/departments/archives/databases/home.html.

Davis, Rodney O. "Private Albert Cashier, As Regarded By His/Her Comrades." *Illinois Historical Journal* 82 (1989), 108–12.

The Dispatch (Moline, Illinois), October 11, 1915.

The Dispatch (Moline, Illinois), October 13, 1915.

"Jennie Becomes Albert To Get Her Rights." *The Pantagraph,* September 25, 1978.

Lannon, Mary Catherine. *Albert D. J. Cashier and the Ninety-Fifth Illinois Infantry (1844–1915).* PhD diss., University of Illinois, 1969.

"Little Albert Cashier Woman Soldier, Insane." *Sioux City Journal,* March 29, 1914.

"Open Albert's Cottage During Pontiac Reunion." *The Pantagraph,* August 30, 1962.

Pepper, Samuel. *My Dear Wife: The Civil War Letters of Private Samuel Pepper Company G–5th Illinois Infantry 1862–1865.* Transcribed and Ed. Franklin R. Crawford. Caledonia, IL: Muffled Drum Press, 2003.

Pepper, Samuel. "Samuel Pepper To His Wife Ophelia, Alabama June 18, 1865." Boone County Museum of History. Belvidere, Illinois.

Reece, J. W. *Report of the Adjutant-General of the State of Illinois Vol. V.* Springfield, IL: Phillips Bros., 1901.

"Soldier Kept Her Secret Well." *The Pantagraph,* May 17, 1950.

"Take Woman Soldier to Insane Asylum." *Oakland Tribune,* March 28, 1914.

Walters, Karen. "Saunemin Welcomes Civil War Secrets Return." *The Pantagraph,* October 2, 2006.

"Woman Civil War Vet Honored." *The Pantagraph,* January 3, 1996.

Wood, Wales, W. *History of the Ninety-Fifth Regiment Illinois Infantry Volunteers.* Chicago: Chicago Tribune Co., 1865.

MARY GALLOWAY (WOUNDED AT ANTIETAM)

Blanton, DeAnne. "Women Soldiers of the Civil War, Part 3." *Prologue,* Spring 1993.

Blanton, DeAnne, and Lauren M. Cook. *They Fought Like Demons: Women Soldiers in the Civil War.* Baton Rouge: Louisiana State University Press, 2002.

Kaminski, Theresa. *Dr. Mary Walker's Civil War: One Woman's Journey to the Medal of Honor and the Fight for Women's Rights.* Guilford, CT: Globe Pequot Press, 2020.

Oates, Stephen B. *A Woman of Valor: Clara Barton and the Civil War.* New York: The Free Press, 1994.

Pryor, Elizabeth Brown. *Clara Barton: Professional Angel.* Philadelphia: University of Pennsylvania Press, 1987.

Schulte, Brigid. "Woman Soldiers Fought, Bled and Died in the Civil War, Then Were Forgotten." Accessed 11/2/2020. https://www.washingtonpost.com/local/women -soldiers-fought-bled-and-died-n-the-civil-war-then-were-forgotten/2013/04/26 /fa722dba-a1a2-11e2-82bc-511538ae90a4_story.html.

FLORENA BUDWIN (WOMAN PRISONER AT ANDERSONVILLE)

Bates, Samuel P. *A Diary of Prison Life: Andersonville and Florence, South Carolina Private Samuel Elliott Co. A 7th Pennsylvania Reserves.* Vol. 1. Harrisburg, PA: B. Singerly, 1869.

Blanton, DeAnne, and Lauren M. Cook. *They Fought Like Demons: Women Soldiers in the Civil War.* Baton Rouge: Louisiana State University Press, 2002.

Florence (SC) Morning News, February 8, 1959.

"The Grave of a Heroine." *Helena Independent,* June 24, 1890.

National Park Service. "Comfortable Camps: Archaeology of the Confederate Guard Camps at the Florence Stockade National Park Service and Florence National Cemetery." Accessed 10/30/2020. https://www.nps.gov/articles/-comfortable -camps-archeology-of-the-confederate-guard-camp-at-the-florence-stockade -teaching-with-historic-places.htm.

National Register of Historic Places: "The Stockade." Accessed 10/30/2020. www
.nationalregister.sc.gov/Florence/s10817721007/s10817721007.pdf.
"A Romantic Episode." Macon Telegraph, November 28, 1888.
Salisbury Carolina Watchman, December 11, 1873.
Singleton, Burt, and Stan Lewis. "Story of a Great Love Amidst Hell and Horror of
Civil War." Charlotte Observer, February 9, 1941.
"A Woman Soldier of the North." New York Times, May 27, 1934.

CATHAY WILLIAMS (WILLIAM CATHAY)

African-American Lives. Eds. Henry Louis Gates Jr. and Evelyn Brooks Higginbotham.
New York: Oxford University Press, 2004.
Blanton, Deanne. "Cathay Williams: Black Woman Soldier, 1866–1868." Minerva 10,
nos. 3-4 (1992).
"Cathay Williams." St. Louis Daily Times, January 2, 1876.
Djossa, Christina Ayele. "The First (Documented) Black Woman to Serve in the U.S.
Army." Accessed 9/18/2020. https://www.atlasobscura.com/articles/cathay
-williams-buffalo-soldier.
Military Compiled Service Records. Civil War. Private William Cathay Service
Records. Record Group 94. National Archives, Washington, DC.
National Park Service. "Cathay Williams." Accessed 7/10/2020. https://www.nps.gov
/people/cwilliams.htm.
National Park Service. "Cathay Williams Primary Sources." Accessed 9/20/2020.
https://www.nps.gov/goga/learn/education/upload/BS_PrimarySources
_2008-01-18_med.pdf.
Rand-Caplan, Ramona. "Cathay Williams." Accessed 7/10/2020. www.blackpast.org
/african-american-history/williams-cathay-1850/.
Tucker, Phillip Thomas. Cathy Williams: From Slave to Buffalo Soldier. Mechanicsburg,
PA: Stackpole Books, 2009.
Wolf, Julie, and Henry Louis Gates Jr. "Cathay Williams: She Pretended To Be a Man
to Enlist as a Buffalo Soldier." Accessed 9/20/2020. https://www.theroot.com
/cathay-williams-she-pretended-to-be-a-man-to-enlist-as-1790858969.

MARY OWENS JENKINS (JOHN EVANS)

Blanton, DeAnne, and Lauren M. Cook. They Fought Like Demons: Women Soldiers in the
Civil War. Baton Rouge: Louisiana State University Press, 2002.
Danville (PA) News, February 3, 1961.
Evening Independent (Massillon, Ohio), May 28, 1937.
Evening Independent (Massillon, Ohio), July 3, 1976.
Grazier, Steven. "Mary Owens Was a Soldier in Union Army Disguised As a Man."
Record Courier, May 29, 2017.
"Honors for Fair Soldier." Pittsburgh Post-Gazette, May 31, 1909.

The Press (Kansas City, Kansas), September 4, 1896.

"Served By Her Lover's Side." *Washington Evening Star*, July 7, 1896.

ELIZABETH "LIZZIE" COMPTON (JOHNNY "JACK" COMPTON)

"Another Female Soldier." Leeds Intelligencer and Yorkshire General Advertiser, January 23, 1864.

Courier-Journal (Louisville, Kentucky), June 2, 1864.

Daily Ohio Statesman (Columbus, Ohio), Friday Morning March 5, 1864.

Devens, R. M. Book of Anecdotes of the Rebellion. St. Louis: J.H. Mason, 1889.

Eggleston, George C. *Southern Soldiers Stories.* New York: McMillian Co., 1898.

Eggleston, Larry G. *Women in the Civil War: Extraordinary Stories of Soldiers, Spies, Nurses, Doctors, Crusaders, and Others.* Jefferson, NC: McFarland and Company, 2003.

Hall, Richard H. *Patriots in Disguise: Women Warriors of the Civil War.* Lawrence: University of Kansas, 2006.

Lansing (MI) *State Republican*, January 13, 1864.

Lossing, Benson. *The Pictorial Field Book of the Civil War in the United States of America.* Vol. III. New Haven, CT: G.S. Lester, 1880.

Rochester Union, March 6, 1864.

Washington Daily Morning Chronicle, February 24, 1864.

SARAH MALINDA PRITCHARD BLALOCK (SAM BLALOCK)

Adams, James T. *26th Regiment North Carolina Infantry.* Accessed 8/24/2020. https:// digital.ncdcr.gov/digital/collection/.

Arthur, John Preston. *A History of Watauga County, North Carolina with Sketches of Prominent Families.* Richmond, VA: Arthur Everett Waddey Co., 1915.

Carolina Journal, March 22, 2012. Accessed 0/30/2020. https://www.carolinajournal .com/opinion-article/linda-and-keith-blalock-a-strange-love-story-of-the-civil -war/.

Gerard, Philip. "The Great Adventure of the Outlaw Blalocks." *Our State Magazine.* Accessed 10/30/2020. https://www.ourstate.com/outlaw-blalocks/.

Hardy, Michael. "Old Watauga and the Civil War." *High Country Magazine*, June 2012.

Hardy, Michael C. "Was William Blalock Imprisoned?" Accessed 10/30/2020. http:// michaelchardy.blogspot.com/2017/05/was-william-blalock-imprisoned.html.

Histories of the Several Regiments and Battalions from North Carolina in the Great War 1861–1865. Ed. Walter Clark. Vol. II. Goldsboro, NC: Nash Brothers, 1901.

Lenoir (NC) *Topic*, October 12, 1887.

Moore, John W. *Roster of North Carolina Troops in the War between the States Vol. II.* Raleigh, NC: Ashe and Gatliy, 1882.

Morning Post (Raleigh, North Carolina), February 11, 1900.

News and Observer (Raleigh, North Carolina), September 18, 1927.

News and Observer (Raleigh, North Carolina), August 27, 1995.

Rocky Mount (NC) *Telegram*, January 30, 1981.

Slappey, Kellie. "Sarah Malinda Pritchard Blalock (1839–1903)." Accessed 10/30/2020. www.northcarolinahistory.org/encylopedia/sarah-malinda-pritchard-blalock -1839-1903/.

Statesville (NC) *Daily Record*, September 24, 1935.

US Bureau of the Census of Population. Washington, DC: Government Printing Office, 1850.

US Bureau of the Census of Population. Washington, DC: Government Printing Office, 1870.

US Bureau of the Census of Population. Washington, DC: Government Printing Office, 1880.

William "Keith" McKesson Blalock Pension Application. Keith Blalock Collection, Appalachian State University Special Collections Research Center, Boone, North Carolina.

SARAH EMMA EDMONDS (FRANKLIN THOMPSON)

Blanton, DeAnne. "Women Soldiers of the Civil War." *Prologue*, Spring 1993.

Blanton, DeAnne, and Lauren M. Cook. *They Fought Like Demons: Women Soldiers in the Civil War*. Baton Rouge: Louisiana State University Press, 2002.

Edmonds, A. Emma E. *Nurse and Spy in the Union Army: Comprising the Adventure and Experience of a Woman in Hospitals, Camps and Battle-fields*. Hartford, CT: W.S. Williams & Co., 1865.

"An Episode of the War." *New York Times*, May 30, 1886.

"Flint Woman One of First To Answer Lincoln's Call." *Ironwood Daily*, February 1, 1961.

History, Art & Archives, US House of Representatives. "The So Very 'Peculiar' Case of Sarah Seelye." Accessed March 20, 2020. https://history.house.gov/Blog/2020 /March/3-20-SarahSeelye/.

"History Repeats Itself As Woman Finds She Must Hide Her Sex." *Baltimore Sun*, September 30, 1991.

Liberty Letters. "Sarah Emma Edmonds a.k.a. Private Franklin Thompson." Accessed 11/10/2020. www.libertyletters.com/resources/civil-war/sarah-emma-edmonds .php.

Logansport (IN) *Pharos-Tribune*, November 11, 1898.

National Park Service. "Sarah Emma Edmonds." Accessed March 20, 2020. www.nps .gov/people/Sarah-emma-edmonds.htm.

"Obituary." *St. Paul Globe*, November 27, 1898.

"A Remarkable Career." *Fort Scott Weekly Monitor*, January 17, 1884.

Robertson, John. *Michigan in the War*. Lansing, MI: W.S. George & Co., 1882.

Sarah Edmonds, Civil War and Later Pension Files; Department of Veterans Affairs, Record Group 15; National Archives, Washington, DC.

Sarah Emma Edmonds Seelye, Sarah Emma Edmonds, "Michigan in Letters: Sarah Emma Edmonds Seelye." Accessed 6/29/2020. www.michiganinletters.org /search/label/seelyesarahemmaedmonds.

"Woman Deserter Asks for a Pension." *New York Times*, March 10, 1884.

Loreta Janeta Velazquez (Harry T. Buford)

Blanton, DeAnne, and Lauren M. Cook. *They Fought Like Demons: Women Soldiers in the Civil War.* Baton Rouge: Louisiana State University Press, 2002.

Cincinnati Enquirer, January 23, 1867.

Civil War Richmond. Accessed 9/26/2020. www.civilwarrichmond.com.

Coski, John. "Loreta Velasquez Letters." Accessed 9/26/2020. www.ACWM.org/blog /July-2016-documents-month-loreta-velasquez-letters/.

Davis, William C. *Inventing Loreta Velasquez: Confederate Soldier Impersonator, Media Celebrity, and Con Artist.* Carbondale: Southern Illinois University Press, 2016.

Hoffert, Sylvia D. "Heroine or Hoaxer." *Civil War Illustrated,* June 1978, Hershey, Pennsylvania.

"Lieutenant Buford." *Chattanooga Daily Rebel,* August 4, 1863.

New Orleans Daily Picayune, January 5, 1867.

Richmond Daily Examiner, September 15, 1863.

"Sent South." *Staunton Spectator,* July 21, 1863.

Velazquez, Loreta Janeta. *The Woman in Battle: A Narrative of the Exploits, Adventures and Travels of Madame Loreta Janeta Velazquez, Otherwise Known as Lieutenant Harry T. Buford, Confederate States Army.* Richmond, VA: Dustin, Gilman & Co., 1876.

"The Woman in Battle." Daily Gazette, May 5, 1877.

Unfinished Lives, Part II

"Alton in the Civil War: Alton Prison." Accessed 11/17/2020. www.altonweb.com /history/civilwar/confed/.

American Battlefield Trust. "Female Soldiers in the Civil War." Accessed 11/4/2020. www.battlefields.org/learn/articles/female-soldiers-civil-war.

Blanton, DeAnne. "Women Soldiers of the Civil War." *Prologue,* Spring 1993.

Blanton, DeAnne, and Lauren M. Cook. *They Fought Like Demons: Women Soldiers in the Civil War.* Baton Rouge: Louisiana State University Press, 2002.

Davis, Robert Scott. *Ghosts and Shadows of Andersonville: Essay on the Secret Social Histories of America's Deadliest Prison.* Macon, GA: Mercer University Press, 2006.

Donaho, Marlea S. *Belle Isle, Point Lookout, the Press and the Government: The Press and Reality of Civil War Camps.* PhD diss., Virginia Commonwealth University, 2017.

Edmonds, Sarah Emma Evlyn. *The Female Spy of the Union Army.* Boston: DeWolfe, Fiske, 1864.

Eggleston, Larry G. *Women in the Civil War: Extraordinary Stories of Soldiers, Spies, Nurses, Doctors, Crusaders, and Others.* Jefferson, NC: McFarland and Company, 2003.

Kerr, Dr. W. J. W. "Sad Ending of a Wedding Trip." *Confederate Veteran,* July 1915, Nashville, Tennessee.

Murphy, Jim. *A Savage Thunder: Antietam and the Bloody Road to Freedom.* New York: Margaret K. McElderry Books, 2009.

National Park Service. "History of the Andersonville Prison." Accessed 11/5/2020. https://www.nps.gov/ande/learn/history/culture/camp_sumter_history.htm.

Pickenpaugh, Roger. *Captives in Blue: The Civil War Prisons of the Confederacy.* Tuscaloosa: University of Alabama Press, 2013.

"Remarkable Incident of the War." *Princeton Clarion*, November 14, 1863.

Stanczak, Christie. "Women at Antietam." National Park Service. Accessed 11/4/2020. https://www.nps.gov/anti/learn/historyculture/women-at-antietam.htm.

State of Ohio. *Official Roster of the Soldiers of the State of Ohio in the War of the Rebellion.* Vol. III. Ohio: Akron, Werner, Co., 1886.

Thiesen, William H. "United States Revenue Cutter Operations in the Civil War." *Naval History Magazine.* Accessed 11/4/2020. https://www.usni.org/magazines/naval-history-magazine/2019/june/us-revenue-cutter-operations-civil-war.

Wakeman, Sarah Rosetta. *An Uncommon Soldier: The Civil War Letters of Sarah Rosetta Wakeman, Alias Pvt. Lyons Wakeman, 153rd Regiment, New York State Volunteers 1862–1864.* Ed. Lauren Cook Burgess. New York: Oxford University Press, 1994.

"Woman Was a Soldier." *Ordway New Era*, September 10, 1909.

About the Author

A. J. SCHENKMAN IS A NEW YORK–BASED WRITER. SINCE HIS START writing for local newspapers, Schenkman has branched out into writing for magazines, blogs, and academic journals, in both history and other subjects. Schenkman is also author of several books about local, national, and regional history.

CPSIA information can be obtained
at www.ICGtesting.com
Printed in the USA
BVHW071213190921
616996BV00003B/3

9 781493 055265